Guide
to use of
DEWEY
Decimal Classification

Guide

to use of

DEWEY

Decimal Classification

Based on the practice of the
Decimal Classification Office
at
The Library of Congress

FOREST PRESS
OF
LAKE PLACID CLUB EDUCATION FOUNDATION

LAKE PLACID CLUB
ESSEX COUNTY, NEW YORK

1962

The numbers and their designated meanings used in this volume are from DEWEY Decimal Classification, Edition 16, © 1958 by Forest Press, Inc.

Library of Congress catalog card number 61–16797

THIS BOOK WAS COMPOSED, PRINTED AND BOUND
IN THE UNITED STATES OF AMERICA
AT KINGSPORT PRESS, INC., KINGSPORT, TENNESSEE

Contents

Contents

Preface

When Melvil Dewey first publisht his Decimal Classification, 85 years
ago, its application to the arrangement of books on shelves or cards in
classified catalogs was relatively simple; so simple that he was able to
leave unused several of the 1,000 three-digit numbers. Since that time the
written record of knowledge has grown enormously, the ideas which must
be represented in a classification have multiplied many times, and the
problems of cataloging and classification, bibliography, and all phases of
information retrieval have become correspondingly more complex. In con-
sequence, great care must now be exercised in applying consistently the
rules of cataloging and classification to the 18,000 heads which have de-
velopt from Melvil Dewey's original 10 classes, 100 divisions, and 1,000
sections, if they are to serve their purposes efficiently and effectively.

During the 85 years since 1876 the DEWEY Decimal Classification has
spread thruout the civilized world and become an indispensable tool for
the organization of knowledge and the records of knowledge in every
field of human endeavor. This has been due first and foremost to the
soundness of the original conception which, with simplest possible notation—the 10 Arabic numerals for the tables, the 26 letters of the Roman
alphabet for the relative index—nevertheless provided unlimited opportunity for expansion; but also to the insistence of the author, editors and
publisher on maintaining firmly the basic principle of *integrity of numbers*, so that meanings once assigned should not be changed except for
the most urgent practical reasons. To adhere to this principle, within the
basic structure of the classification, while meeting the insistent demands
of the other equally basic, and frequently conflicting, principle of *keep-
ing pace with knowledge*, calls for the highest type of editorial talent,
guided by professionally establisht criteria and controlled by consistent
office procedures.

For the classifier, the *user* of the classification, this *Guide* seeks to provide the nearest equivalent to the experience, criteria and procedures
which guide the editor, the *maker* of the classification. It is to be hoped
that its availability will minimize the need, real or supposed, for local
modifications or distortions of the publisht schedules (other than variations authorized in the text) which cut the user off from the currently

available experience and recommendations of the Editorial Office and the internationally understood meanings of the Arabic numbers, regardless of language, thruout the world. Avoidance of such unorthodox departures is doubly desirable in that the *making* of a classification is a far more complex matter than the *user* generally realizes, so that amateur tinkering often creates more problems than it solves.

The form of the *Guide* is concise and practical rather than theoretical or historical. Its scope is:

1. To synthesize instructions in existing editions and formulate a set of rules for DC practice.
2. To provide specific rules for books the contents of which do not conform to the general classification schemes.
3. To describe practical deviations from the general rules.
4. To provide explanation of technical terms used in the schedules of existing editions.
5. To describe general principles and procedures for determining length of numbers, application of form divisions, etc.
6. To indicate practical methods of adjusting schedules to meet local needs without upsetting the basic scheme or blocking future development.

Random examples of the help to be expected from this *Guide* might include:

1. Should I class a book dealing about half-and-half with lion hunting specifically and with big game hunting generally with the broader or the narrower subject?
2. Should a work on the U.S. public debt go in 336.340 973 or in 336.73?
3. Obligations of church to state: 322 or 261.7? Obligations of state to church?
4. Does the effect of Florentine Renaissance writers on Elizabethan writers go with Italian or English literature?
5. Suppose I have a book on the physical laws of the transformation of heat into mechanical energy, on the theory of the steam engine, and on the application of steam engines to electric power generation; does it belong in 536.7, in 621.11, in 621.312 132, or elsewhere?
6. Where goes a book dealing with the history, use, and manufacture of gloves?
7. What about one on tobacco, its botany, cultivation, commercial products, use, hygiene, ethics?

Preface

The *Guide* supplements but does not repeat the basic general rules included in the introduction to each edition. It makes reference to other classification tools, such as Mann and Merrill, intended as aids to DC, but stands on its own feet as part of the DC system it is intended to support.

Small public, school, and private libraries will profit by its enunciation of general principles. Larger general libraries will need it in general practice. It will serve many needs of special and reference libraries. It will be particularly helpful to library schools, their teachers and students. Teaching and training in classification leading to a degree in library science will be made both easier and more certain. With DC becoming worldwide in its use, many of the common barriers of language, customs and religion will not seem so forbidding with the *Guide* available.

Forest Press of Lake Placid Club Education Foundation, the nonprofit institution to which Melvil Dewey entrusted the publication, future development and perpetuation of the Decimal Classification, presents with pride and pleasure this latest addition to the tools and techniques of classification.

Godfrey Dewey
PRESIDENT, FOREST PRESS, INC.

Lake Placid Club
New York
30 June 1961

Foreword

The Decimal Classification Editorial Policy Committee welcomes this *Guide* as a further service of the Decimal Classification Office and the Forest Press to the users of the Dewey Decimal Classification. No classification can be so explicit and self-sufficient as automatically to produce uniform and consistent results when applied to the infinite variety of books. Hence there has been a long-felt need for explanation of the practices of the Decimal Classification Office in particular situations, and guidance in the application of the Classification to books not covered by Library of Congress cards.

The long experience of Miss Pressey and Miss Kenton in classifying the wide range of materials added to the Library of Congress over a period of thirty years is here made available to other libraries. It is our hope and our belief that this experience will be of value to all users of the Dewey Decimal Classification.

The present members of the Committee are Elizabeth C. Borden, Edwin B. Colburn, Godfrey Dewey, Virginia Drewry, Carlyle J. Frarey, Harriet D. MacPherson, Lucile M. Morsch, Pauline A. Seely, and Wyllis E. Wright.

Wyllis E. Wright
CHAIRMAN, DECIMAL CLASSIFICATION
EDITORIAL POLICY COMMITTEE

Williams College Library
Williamstown, Massachusetts
30 June 1961

Introduction

History

The need for a guide to the use of the Dewey Decimal Classification has been recognized for many years. The opportunity to produce one presented itself when, after the completion of Edition 16 of the Classification (1958) and Abridged Edition 8 (1959), the responsibilities of the Library of Congress for editing and applying the DC were combined in the newly created Decimal Classification Office. Plans were accordingly presented to the Decimal Classification Editorial Policy Committee, and suggestions for the content of the "manual" (as it was then called) were invited from the library community.

Scope

After giving careful consideration to the needs to be met and to the literature already available to meet it, the Committee decided that the *Guide* should be concise and practical rather than theoretical or historical, based primarily on the use made of the Classification by the DC Office and by libraries that follow its practices. The Committee felt that specific references should be made chiefly to Edition 16 but that the requirements of users of other editions should be considered, and that the *Guide* need not repeat information given in the Classification since it could be used only in conjunction with the DC schedules. Hence this book does not attempt to deal with the theoretical basis of the DC, with the history of the development of the schedules, or with the persons involved in them, interesting tho it might be to deal with these subjects. It does, however, include brief history notes to enable classifiers to understand some of the DC numbers on earlier Library of Congress printed cards. Because it is primarily a guide to the Classification as used by this Office, it largely excludes the many variations authorized by the introduction and schedules of Edition 16 as well as the vast number that have been adopted by libraries to meet individual needs. The examples cited are taken from Edition 16 and, in a very few cases, from its supplement, *Decimal Classification Additions, Notes, and Decisions*, v. 1 (1959–   ).

An exhaustive code covering every conceivable problem would run to greater length than Edition 16 itself, and it would grow still longer thru the daily application of the DC. In order to hold the *Guide* to manageable size, each entry's potential usefulness to classifiers has been considered carefully. Tho the *Guide*'s contents are selective, it will aid in the solution of other problems thru the use of analogy and thru the application of general principles.

Index

The *Guide* has no index. This feature is rendered unnecessary because of the arrangement by DC numbers (access to which is supplied by the relative index of the various editions of the DC), the many references between entries, and the summary table of contents for the section entitled "General Principles and Procedures."

"History" Notes

Most entries labeled "History" point out practices formerly followed by the DC Office which differ from those currently employed, tho no formal relocation has been shown in the Classification schedules. ("Relocation" in its formal sense is the reassignment, between one edition of the DC and its successor, of a specific topic from a given number to another number which differs from the first in respects other than length.) "History" notes are significant in relation to Library of Congress cards bearing numbers supplied from earlier editions of the DC. The following editions have been used:

Edition 6, 1899   Used in supplying numbers which appeared on cards for works included in the *A.L.A. Catalog 1904*. Most of these cards have been reprinted in revised form, with DC numbers from later editions.

Edition 12, 1927   Used April 1930–September 1932.

Edition 13, 1932   Used October 1932–Summer 1942. Supplemented by *Notes and Decisions on the Application of "Decimal Clasification, Edition 13,"* no. 1, February 1934–no. 15, April 1942.

Edition 14, 1942   Used Summer 1942–November 1958. Supplemented by *Notes and Decisions on the Application of the Decimal Classification,* Second Series, no. 1, July 1942–no. 38, October 1951.

Edition 15, 1952   Used January 1952–November 1958, concurrently with Edition 14. Supplemented by *Notes and Decisions on the Application of the Decimal Classification,* Third Series, no. 1, January 1952–nos. 12 & 13, October 1954 & January 1955.

Introduction

Edition 16, 1958   Used since December 1958. Supplemented by *Decimal Classification Additions, Notes, and Decisions,* v. 1, no. 1, January 1959+

Abridged Edition 8, 1959   Used since May 1961 for works written for children.

A few entries labeled "History" are included to assist in understanding a part of the schedules rather than to point out changes in practice. *Example:* 660's–680's *History.*

Acknowledgments

It is always a pleasure to give public notice of indebtedness. This *Guide,* like other editorial operations of the DC Office, owes its promotion and much of its financial support to the abiding interest in the Dewey Decimal Classification that is manifested by the directors of Forest Press, Inc., Verner W. Clapp, Deo B. Colburn, Godfrey Dewey, Walter A. Hafner, and Howard Haycraft. It owes its practical and concise form to the guidance of the Decimal Classification Editorial Policy Committee, the names of whose members appear in the "Foreword." It owes its prestige as a service of the Library of Congress to other libraries to the support of Librarian L. Quincy Mumford and Chief Assistant Librarian Rutherford D. Rogers. It owes its timely undertaking and completion to the driving insistence of LC's Processing Department Director, John W. Cronin, that, if the work were not done now, it might never be done.

Most of all, it owes its very being to the members of the DC Office staff: to Dorothy Fauntleroy Gover, Marie Molnar Henshaw, Elva L. Krogh, Ruby York Weinbrecht, and Elsie Kresge Yoder for numerous contributions both intellectual and manual; and to those two who know more about the use of the DC than anyone else, Alice M. Kenton and Julia C. Pressey, who have crowned their 30 years each in the Decimal Classification Office and earned plaudits to cheer them in their imminent retirement by performing the lion's share of the responsible work.

Benjamin A. Custer
EDITOR, DEWEY DECIMAL CLASSIFICATION

Decimal Classification Office
The Library of Congress
Washington 25, D.C.
28 June 1961

General Principles and Procedures

I. Situations not covered This *Guide* is exactly that: a guide. Books are as individual and as diverse as their authors, and no set of principles and rules will cover the classification of all of them. For practical purposes, the classifier must sometimes judiciously ignore the letter of what follows while still observing its spirit

II. Doubtful situations Sometimes it is exceedingly difficult for the classifier to decide into which of two or more numbers a work should go. In such cases, it is likely that it may be placed with equal usefulness in either or any one of the numbers. Notes in this *Guide* reading, "When in doubt prefer . . ." are intended to help in such situations

III. Evaluations In theory, it is not the province of the classifier to serve as literary or artistic critic or as judge of the value or accuracy of a work. In practice, however, the classifier sometimes is compelled to make such judgments in order to decide in which of two or more numbers a work is best placed. Points to consider are described under certain numbers in the pages that follow, *e.g.*, **040's B, 700's C**

IV. Most specific subject Class a work in the most specific number that will contain its subject; then, if its subject is limited geographically, and if the number is specifically for that subject, and if the schedules permit, add subdivision for place; or, if the subject is limited by other form, add appropriate form division. Except in the 800's the general rule is to class first by most specific subject, second by place, and third by form of presentation. Note that, except where there is specific provision for it, as in the 800's, authorship is not a proper basis for classification, *e.g.*, United Nations publications on social welfare 360's *not* 341.13+

See also **Form Divisions A**

v. **Subjects in context**

A   Before placing a work in a number, survey the entry for which that number stands in relation to (1) the superordinate entries under which it falls, (2) the coordinate entries which stand beside it, (3) the subordinate entries which fall under it

(1) Looking back thru the hierarchy of ever broader entries helps to make clear the aspect of the immediate subject which is intended. Remember that headings, notes, references which apply to a broad subject apply equally to all its parts. *Example:* 633.15 Corn is under 633.1 Cereals and grains, which is under 633 Field crops, which is under 633–635 Production of specific crops, which is under 630 Agriculture, which is under 600 Technology (Applied science); therefore, 633.15 is used for corn as a cereal field crop and not as a garden vegetable (as indicated in the reference from 633 to 635), and it includes harvesting, varieties, yield, storage of the crop (as indicated in the note under 633–635), and it treats of the agricultural techniques of raising corn rather than the scientific description of the plant (as indicated in the reference from 633–635 to 582–589)

(2) Looking at coordinate entries helps to define and discriminate clearly between them and the number under consideration. *Example:* Consideration of 633 Field crops, 634 Fruit crops, and 635 Garden crops, and of the notes and references under them, helps to define the exact meaning of each

(3) Looking down thru the subdivisions of an entry helps to delimit its scope, and to make certain that the most specific possible number has been chosen. *Example:* The subdivisions of 633, 634, and 635 help to show the exact coverage of each

B Note that length of number *usually* shows coordination and subordination, *e.g.,*

550	Earth sciences
551	Geophysics
551.4	Geomorphology and physical geography
551.46	Oceanography
551.461	Atlantic Ocean

But not always; only indention *always* shows coordination and subordination, *e.g.,*

551.461	Atlantic Ocean
551.464	Southern Atlantic Ocean
972	Mexico
972.1	Northern states
972.7	Southern Pacific states
972.8	Central America
972.81	Guatemala

VI. More than one subject

A (1) If a work deals with two subjects, class it with the subject given greater emphasis, *e.g.,* class the effect of one subject on another with the subject affected. (2) If the emphasis on the two subjects is about equal, class the work with the subject treated first in the work. (3) If emphasis is about equal and both subjects are treated concurrently, class the work with the subject coming first in the schedules, unless the schedules themselves provide otherwise

B If a work deals with three or more subjects, follow preceding principles; however, modify (2)–(3) as follows: if emphasis is about equal but the subjects are all subdivisions of one broader subject, class the work with the broader subject

VII. Contrasting opinions or systems If a work gives about equal attention to two different opinions or systems but advocates one of them, class it with the one advocated. However, if the work gives greater emphasis to one than to the other, class with the one more emphasized, without respect to advocacy, in accordance with **General Principles VI A** (1). *Examples:* Class in **321.8** a work dealing about equally with modern dictatorship and modern democracy but advocating the latter; in **282** a work by a Protestant criticizing and emphasizing the Roman Catholic Church

VIII. More than one aspect Frequently a work deals with (1) the theory of or basic principles behind a process or procedure, (2) its technique, and (3) its application to a specific subject; *e.g.,* electrodynamics **537.6**, electrodynamic machinery **621.313**, electric locomotives **625.263**. If theory and technique are preliminary or introductory to the application, and the author's purpose is to describe the application (to which, in such cases, at least a third of the work's bulk is usually devoted), class with the application. But if the "application" is only an example (with much less space given to it), and the author's purpose is to describe the theory or the technique, class with the theory or technique

IX. Comprehensive works

 A "Comprehensive works" as applied to a number in the schedules of Edition 16 and in this *Guide* has two distinct meanings:

  (1) The number includes not only works dealing with the subject in its context, but also broader works. (*See* **General Principles V A.**)

(a) The added content may consist of other aspects of the same subject, that is, parts of the subject which, if dealt with separately, would belong in different contexts and, therefore, in different numbers. *Examples:* 1. 331.833 Housing. The context of this number (under 331.83 Health, welfare, recreation facilities, under 331.8 Industrial sociology, under 331 Labor economics) shows that the primary subject is housing for the working class as a contribution to industrial welfare. But the "comprehensive works" note shows that the number includes also broader works on housing that deal with this aspect and other aspects together, and the cross references show where these other aspects may be found when dealt with separately: hygienic aspects in 613.5, planning aspects in 711.58, and so on. 2. 669 Metallurgy. The primary subject of this number and its subdivisions, as defined by the first note, is production of metals from ore and scrap. But the note "comprehensive works on metals" shows that the number and its subdivisions include also broader works on metals that deal with the metallurgic aspect and other aspects together, and the cross references show where these other aspects may be found when dealt with separately: mining aspects in 622.34, manufacture of metal products in 671–673, and so on

(b) Or, the added content may consist of one or more different but related subjects which, tho frequently written about in conjunction with the primary subject, would, if dealt with separately, belong in different numbers. *Examples:* 1. 331.11 Employment. This is a subject which is often written about in conjunction with unemployment. The "comprehensive works" note shows that the number includes, in addition to the primary subject, broader works on both employment and unemployment, and the cross reference shows that unemployment when considered separately may be found in 331.13. 2. 531 Mechanics of solids. This is a subject which is often written about in conjunction with mechanics of liquids and mechanics of gases. The "comprehensive works" note shows that the number includes, in addition to the primary subject, broader works dealing with all the parts of mechanics, and the cross references show where the other parts of mechanics may be found when considered separately: liquids in 532.1, gases in 533

(2) The number includes works that deal with the subject as a whole or with many parts of it, but at least *some* (and in many cases *all*) the specific parts when dealt with separately fall in other numbers that are not subdivisions of the given number. *Examples:* 1. 331.7 Economic aspects of specific occupations and professions. The "comprehensive works" note shows that in this number and its subdivisions go works dealing with all or several parts of the subject, but the cross references show that certain parts, when dealt with individually, belong elsewhere: unemployment in 331.137 8, earnings in 331.28, hours in 331.818. Since there are no other references, it follows that other parts, even when dealt with separately, fall here, *e.g.*, employment, economic advantages. 2. 631.5 Crop production. The "comprehensive works" note shows that in this number and its subdivisions go works dealing with these operations as applied to all or many kinds of specific crops, but the cross reference shows that works dealing separately with production of any specific crop belong elsewhere. This is a "blanket" reference, and it exhausts all the separate crops, no one of which, separately considered, is left here. 3. 670 Manufactures. The "comprehensive works" note shows that in this number go works dealing with all or many kinds of manufactures. Many specific manufactures, when dealt with individually, fall in subdivisions of this number, *e.g.*, paper and pulp 676; but the cross references show that certain other specific manufactures fall elsewhere

B   In classing an apparently comprehensive work on a subject, be sure that it is, indeed, comprehensive. If the emphasis is on some one aspect or part of the subject, class with that aspect or part, *e.g.*, class a work on various aspects of ferrous metals but emphasizing the manufacture of products in 672 *not* 669.1, class a work on various economic aspects of the occupation of electrical engineer but emphasizing the earnings in 331.282 13 *not* 331.762 13

C   If the work is, indeed, comprehensive but fails to deal with the specific aspect which falls within the context of the number where the note appears, class it elsewhere, *e.g.*, class a comprehensive work on mechanics of liquids and gases in 532 *not* 531, class a comprehensive work on automation which includes economic and engineering aspects but not sociological in 338.45 *not* 301.243

D   In classing a work dealing comprehensively with many or varied aspects of a specific subject without emphasis on any one, when there is no indication in the schedules or index as to treatment of comprehensive works on that subject, apply the following principles:

(1) Class in the number for the use of an article works dealing comprehensively with its use, history, and manufacture

(2) Class truly comprehensive works on a substance appearing in nature, such as air or water, in the number for the phenomenon in that context in which man first becomes aware of it. *Example:* Class in 551.5 a truly comprehensive work on air, its composition, properties, uses, contamination, effect on plants and animals, aerodynamics, aeronautics

(3) If no other principle is applicable, class a comprehensive work with the aspect the number for which comes first in the schedules. *Examples:* Class in the appropriate subdivisions of 301 comprehensive works covering sociological, economic, scientific, and technological aspects of a subject; in subdivisions of 338, those covering economic, scientific, and technological aspects; in

25

subdivisions of 500, those covering both scientific and technological aspects

See also 900's **B**

x. Number building

A   The instruction, "Divide like" something else, may appear under a single number, *e.g.*, 330.9, 225, 016, or under a series of numbers in a single entry, *e.g.*, 554–559, 974.201–974.204. It may direct the classifier to divide a single number like another single number, *e.g.*, 225 like 220, or like a series, *e.g.*, 330.9 like 930–999; or a series like another series, *e.g.*, 554–559 like 940–999. Note that, when divided, even single numbers become series, *e.g.*, 330.9 becomes 330.91–330.99, 225 ·becomes 225.1–225.9. Every such instruction, therefore, means divide one sequence of numbers (the "primary" sequence) like another sequence (the "secondary" sequence). The procedure follows: (1) Determine and set down that part of the secondary sequence which is appropriate to the work in hand. (2) Cancel all those digits at the left of this number which are common to every number in the secondary sequence (there may be none). (3) Set down those digits of the primary sequence which are common to every number in it, *e.g.*, 330.9, 225, 016, 55, 974.20. (4) Set down the digits left uncanceled from operation (2) to the right of the digits resulting from operation (3). (5) Be sure that a decimal point follows the third digit of the resulting number, and that it does not end in a 0 to the right of the decimal point. *Examples* (in which, for convenience, cancellation is effected by enclosure in curves): (a) In order to class economic conditions in Canada, divide 330.9 like 930–999:

(1) History of Canada   971
(2)   (9)71
(3) 330.9
(4) 330.971

(b) In order to class geology of Iceland, divide 554–559 like 940–999:

(1) History of Iceland   949.1
(2)   (9)49.1
(3) 55
(4) 55491
(5) 554.91

(c) In order to class an exegesis of the New Testament, divide 225 like 220:

(1) Exegesis of Bible   220.6
(2)   (220.)6
(3) 225
(4) 2256
(5) 225.6

(d) In order to class colonial period of New Hampshire history, divide 974.201–974.204 like 974.101–974.104:

(1) Colonial period of Maine history   974.102
(2)   (974.10)2
(3) 974.20
(4) 974.202

(e) In order to class a bibliography of agriculture, divide 016 like 000–999:

(1) Agriculture   630
(2)   630 [no digits common to entire sequence]
(3) 016
(4) 016630
(5) 016.63

B Note that division of any number like other numbers, especially like 000–999, is likely to bring about conflicts and unused subdivisions. *Examples:* 330.193 11 and 330.195 1 are unlikely to be used, because the relationship of statistical methods (311) and mathematics (510) to economics is usually in the field of methodology and therefore better placed in 330.18 and 330.182 respectively

XI. Seldom-used numbers

A   Note that certain numbers in the schedules are seldom if ever used, their chief function being to serve as devices for expanding the schedules: (1) numbers whose subdivisions cover such mutually exclusive topics that few if any works would or could deal with all, or even most, of them, *e.g.*, Form Division 08; (2) numbers whose subdivisions are on such unrelated topics that few if any works are likely to be written on those topics jointly, *e.g.*, history of Paraguay and Uruguay 989

B   Note that, while some numbers are expanded in greater detail than is likely to be needed under the subjects where the expansions appear, the subdivisions will probably be needed where another subject is divided like the first, *e.g.*, details of 611 may be needed under 616.994 and 616.995

XII. Translations and adaptations

Note that a *translation* from one language to another restates the work with little or no change in the meaning and form of the work, and goes with the original work even where, as in the 030's, classification is based on language. An *adaptation* modifies the original work in form, scope, presentation, and possibly language, and, depending upon the amount and kind of modification, may or may not go with the original. Note that a prose translation of poetry is not treated as an adaptation even tho the form is changed. *Examples:* a work of fiction translated from German into English 833+; Dante's *Divine Comedy* translated into German prose 851.1; a scientific work rewritten for younger readers but covering the same field as the original with the original; a novel rewritten for presentation as a play with drama of the language of the play

XIII. Government publications   Be alert to class each government publication according to its true subject. The following types may prove especially troublesome: (1) *Hearings* of United States Congressional committees are background material for consideration of the Congress in its work. Hearings on appropriation bills usually are, in effect, about the organization and work of the department or bureau involved, and go with the organization and management of the department or bureau. Hearings on nominations for an office usually deal with the work of the department or office, and go with its organization and management; but they may be so personal in relation to the life and personality of the candidate that they go with his biography. (2) Hearings usually are followed by *committee reports,* which make proposals that may or may not be enacted. *See* **General Principles XIV.** (3) Hearings and reports may result in the passage of *laws. See* **Form Division 026**

XIV. Proposals and plans   A work dealing with proposals or plans for an object or action goes with the object or action even if the proposals or plans are not actually carried out. *Examples:* proposals for administration of the United States Department of State 353.1, its actual administration 353.1; proposed but not yet implemented plans for conservation of the waters of the Potomac Valley 333.910 975 2

XV. Microreproductions   Note that microreproductions of works (*e.g.,* microfilms, Microcards, Microprints) are not audio-visual aids, but are the works themselves in special form. Class a microreproduction as if it were the original work. Specific libraries have their own systems for designating locations so that each kind of microreproduction may be stored according to its own physical characteristics. Class microreproductions of several works in 081, 082, or in Form Divisions 081–082 under appropriate numbers. Class works about microreproductions in 778.315 if on photographic technique, in 655.32 if on printing technique, in 099 if comprehensive. Class bibliographies of microreproductions with bibliography, *e.g.,* bibliographies of medical works 016.61, bibliographies not limited by subject 016.099

XVI. **Indexes**   Class an index to works on a specific subject with bibliography of the subject; but class an index to a specific work or series of works with the work or series

XVII. **Periodicals and organizations**   Note that periodicals and organizations, including business firms, may change their scopes over a series of years. Class each specific title according to the scope of the periodical or organization as revealed in the first issue of the title received for classification; if in doubt between two numbers, prefer the broader

XVIII. **Textbooks**   Since these are treatises on a subject and useful as such, even if they include such aids to students and teachers as questions, problems, and references, class them with their respective subjects without form division. *See* **Form Division 02; 372.3–372.8 A**

XIX. **Persons who change nationality, country of residence, or orientation**   In those parts of the classification where the choice of a number is dependent in part on a person's nationality, country of residence, or other orientation, *e.g.*, in literature (W. H. Auden's poetry in 821.912 or 811.52?), in art (J. A. McN. Whistler's painting in 759.13 or 759.2 or 759.4?), in biography (J. H. Newman in 922.342 or 922.242?), a practical expedient for determination of the number to be used is (1) to class works by or about a person in a number based on his nationality, country, or orientation at the time the first work is received for classification, and (2) to continue the use of that number for both earlier and later works. However, if at a later time strong or significant qualities, influence, or bias toward another country or orientation become discernible, (3) class works in a new number based on the new situation

XX. **Monuments and memorials**
    A   Class a memorial intended for a specific purpose in addition to commemoration with that purpose, *e.g.*, George Washington Memorial Bridge **624.550 974 72**

B   Class a monument the main purpose of which is to commemorate a war or an event in a war with the war or the event, *e.g.*, Bunker Hill Monument 973.331 2

C   Class the history or description of a monument not included in **A** or **B** with the history or description of the place in which it is located, *e.g.*, history of Washington Monument, Washington, D.C. 975.3

D   Class a specific aspect of a memorial with the aspect, *e.g.*, sculpture of Lincoln statue in Lincoln Memorial, Washington, D.C. 730.973

XXI. Reduction   If the numbers taken from the schedules or built thru the use of "divide like" notes are longer, or result in more detailed classification of any given subject, than a specific library needs, they may be cut or reduced to conform to that library's needs. In cutting, consider the following principles: (1) Do not cut a number to less than three digits. (2) Except for three-digit numbers, do not terminate a number in 0. (3) Cut at a reasonable spot, *i.e.*, one which will bring about a useful grouping of subjects. This is especially applicable to numbers built thru dividing like other numbers. *Example:* 331.28 Wages in specific occupations. Either cut to 331.28 and use the "If preferred" note, or decide on a length of number which will bring about a reasonable grouping, *e.g.*, perhaps one or two digits beyond the base number, with the possibility of more when needed. This would group together in 331.281 78 salaries of musicians, whether singers, orchestra conductors, or violinists; and in 331.287 wages of factory workers regardless of the product manufactured by them. (4) Record in the library's official copy of the schedules all decisions for reduction. See Dewey Decimal Classification, Abridged Edition 8, p. 17–19, for suggestions as to such recording; note that one must be especially cautious in cutting numbers whose length is irregular with respect to coordination and subordination (*see* **General Principles v B**)

Form Divisions

Form Divisions

A   Form divisions are identified by digits which may be added after a subject number, the 0 which introduces them indicating a different kind of basis for subdivision. They are used to bring together works presenting a subject in a special form, *e.g.*, dictionaries. Altho they are known as *form* divisions (and most of them, *e.g.*, handbooks, dictionaries, periodicals, are true forms), some of them, *e.g.*, philosophy, study and teaching, history, are more properly *subject* divisions, and are so considered in application of the general rule of most specific subject (*see* **General Principles** IV). If two "form" divisions are equally applicable to a given work, prefer that of a subject nature, *e.g.*, class dictionaries of the philosophy of a subject in Form Division 01 *not* 03. However, unless the schedules indicate otherwise, prefer Form Divisions 026, 058, 061–063, 071 1–071 2, each of which has geographic subdivision, over Form Division 09

B   So that possible future subject expansion may not be impeded, avoid using a form division if the subject of the work does not have its own specific number, *e.g.*, handbooks of wedding etiquette 395.220 2, but handbooks of etiquette for children 395.1

C   Usually only one 0 is required to introduce a form division, but sometimes two or even three are necessary when the usual single-0 number has been given a different meaning in the schedules. Edition 16 indicates in the schedules the most significant places where two or more 0's are needed, *e.g.*, under 352

D   Note that, when some but not all of the usual form division numbers are given special meanings, the rest of the series may be used with normal form division meanings, unless the schedules state otherwise. *Example:* 500–509, where 501–508.2, 509 have normal meanings, 508.3–508.9 have special meanings, and 500.83–500.86 are printed with two

0's. In some cases it may be desirable—especially where there is prospect that more or all of the single-0 divisions eventually will have special meanings (as with period divisions in history)—to use two 0's thruout for the form divisions. But note also that what seems like a special meaning is in reality often only an extension of the regular form division meaning, in which case the form division should be used with its normal meaning and its normal notation. *Example:* Include in 510.78 not only computation instruments and machines but also other equipment for study, teaching, use

E   Note that form division meanings sometimes are given to numbers that do not have regular form division notation, *e.g.*, thruout 510's and 530's recurrent special provision is made for problems and tables. This feature occurs especially frequently under numbers with geographic subdivision, normally shown by the addition of 09+ but often given special provision; *e.g.*, 372.9 divided like 930–999 where there is a 9 but no 0 before the addition of the numbers showing place; and 373.3–373.9 where there is neither 9 nor 0. In such cases, unless otherwise indicated, the general principles for use of form divisions apply. *Example:* general works on geology of the United States 557.3, but economic geology of the United States 553.097 3

F   Note that the Office does not add form divisions (1) to numbers more than five digits long, (2) to form subdivisions (but it does add them to numbers which contain 0's but are not form divisions, *e.g.*, 301, 621.01), (3) to geographic subdivisions either based on Form Division 09 or provided for in the schedules in some other way, *e.g.*, 372.9, 373.3–373.9, 914–919. *See also* 920's A

G   *History*   Before Edition 13 printed the form division tables with one, two, and three 0's the Office used where applicable the tables printed under 330 and 630. The full tables of "common subdivisions" as printed in Edition 13 were followed until *Notes and Decisions*, Second Series, No. 2, October 1942, stated that the Office was discontinuing the use, except when they were printed in the schedules, of subdivisions of 076, 082, 083 except 083 8, and 088; of geographic subdivisions; of 00 Viewpoints; and of 000 Miscellaneous common subdivisions. Edition 16 continues most of these practices. Before Edition 16 the Office did not add form divisions to history period subdivisions or to local history numbers

See also 000's; 620.01–620.09; 930–999 Form Divisions

Form Division 01   Include here theories, principles, techniques of criticism of a work or works; but class with the work or works criticized the criticism itself. *Examples:* Class in 750.1 esthetics, principles of criticism of painting, but in 759.4 critical appraisal of modern French painting; class in 801.9 theories of literary criticism, but in 811.52 criticism of Robert Frost's poetry. *Exception:* criticism of musical compositions; *see* 780's

See also Form Divisions A; 000's

Form Division 014   Class here works about the terminology of a subject, *i.e.,* its system, etymology, abbreviations, and the like; but class in Form Division 03 lists of words and their meanings

Form Division 02   Include textbooks here only if they are outlines or digests, not if they are treatises

See also General Principles xviii; 000's

Form Division 024   The Office has never used this number to separate works written for children. Since May 1961 numbers from Abridged Edition 8, preceded by **j,** have been used for children's literature

Form Division 026
A   Because this division was not introduced until Edition 16, there are many numbers in the tables, inherited from earlier

editions, which make specific provision of another sort for laws and regulations on a subject, *e.g.*, 021.89, 368.9, 614.09 and thruout the 380's. *See* **Form Divisions E**

B   Note that it is redundant to use Form Division 026 under numbers intended primarily for control by means of laws or government regulations, *e.g.*, **614.83**

See also **Form Divisions A**

Form Division 03   *See* **Form Divisions A; Form Division 014; 000's**

Form Division 05   *See* **Form Divisions 061–063 A; 000's**

Form Division 058   *See* **Form Divisions A**

Form Division 059   Class here only those annuals which have such almanac characteristics as calendars, weather predictions, information about special days

Form Division 06   Note that "foundations" may usually be treated as organizations (**062**), "symposiums" as conferences (**063**)

See also **000's**

Form Divisions 061–063
A   Class here works about an organization, society, or conference. This includes its administrative and business reports, and its bulletins and transactions when these contain lists of officers and members, reports of business meetings, committees, and the like. Class in Form Division **05** or **08** bulletins and transactions which do not contain these features and are, therefore, periodicals or collections about the subject rather than about the organization

B   Note that these form divisions are not used with a number unless the general subject scope of the organization is approximately the same in extent as the subject which that number represents, *e.g.*, Cataloging and Classification Section of American Library Association **025.306 273**; but a conference on subject headings sponsored by that Section and held in Chicago 025.330 063 773 11 *not* 025.306 273, and a collection of papers read at that conference 025.330 082

See also **Form Divisions A**

Form Divisions 061–062

A   Class the local branch of an organization with the parent organization, *e.g.*, Boston branch of a nongovernment United States organization 062 73 *not* 062 744 6

B   Include here conferences of societies having permanent or continuing organizations; but class in 063 meetings having temporary organizations created primarily for planning, administering, reporting the meetings, *e.g.*, symposiums, seminars

Form Division 061   *See* **353–354 A**

Form Divisions 061 1, 062 1, 063 1   Class in these numbers those organizations and conferences that cover more than one continent or parts of more than one, or two or more countries that cannot be drawn together under a single geographic number, *e.g.*, a nongovernment organization covering both the United Kingdom and the United States 062 1 but a nongovernment organization covering several European countries 062 4

Form Division 061 1   Class here international organizations whose delegates are appointed by the member governments, but in 062 1 those among whose delegates are both governmental and nongovernmental appointees

Form Division 062 1   *See* **Form Division 061 1**

Form Divisions 062 3–062 9

A   For geographic subdivision use the area covered by the membership. If the membership varies or is diverse, or if the organization is an institution or foundation without membership as such, use the place of headquarters

B   Since most historical societies draw their membership from and have their headquarters within the area which is the subject of their study and actions, it is redundant to add geographic subdivision after 062, *e.g.*, Minnesota Historical Society 977.600 62 *not* 977.600 627 76

Form Division 063   *See* **Form Divisions 061–062 B**

Form Divisions 063 3–063 9   For geographic subdivision use the specific place where the conference or symposium is held

Form Division 065   *See* **338.1–338.4; 385–388 B**

Form Division 069   Include here works on the subject as an occupation or profession, including qualifications required

Form Division 07   *See* **000's**

Form Divisions 071 1–071 2   *See* **Form Divisions A**

Form Division 074   *See* **914–919 D**

Form Division 076   *See* **Form Divisions G; 351.3; 793.74–793.8**

Form Division 079   Include here "orders" or societies whose main purpose is to grant awards, such as medals, in a specific subject field

Form Division 08   Include here papers or addresses compiled from periodicals or elsewhere; collections of papers written specifically for a book; papers, bulletins, etc., of a society which are about the subject and not about the society

   See also **General Principles XI A; Form Divisions 061–063 A; 000's**

Form Divisions 081–082   *See* **General Principles XV**

Form Division 081   *See* **780's**

Form Divisions 082–083   *See* **Form Divisions G**

Form Division 082   *See* **800's Form Divisions**

Form Division 083   *See* **641.5**

Form Division 084   *See* **700's C**

Form Division 09   Note that this includes the subject limited by locality as well as its history

> *See also* **Form Divisions A; 000's; 332.1–332.3; 385–388 B; 700's B; 800's Form Divisions; 909, 930–999; 914–919 A**

Form Divisions 090 2–090 3   *See* **190's**

000 General Works

000's   Compare the Divisions of this Class with the two-digit form divisions. Note that 030, 050 and 070, 060, 040 and 080, when limited by subject, go with the subject, using Form Divisions 03, 05, 06, and 08, respectively. Divisions 010 and 020 have within themselves provision for subject limitation, *e.g.*, 016 and 026 each divided like 000–999, while Form Division 016 provides an alternative possibility for classing bibliographies limited by subject with the subject. Note that Form Divisions 01, 07, and 09 have no counterparts in this Class, general works on philosophy, education, and history being provided for in 100, 370, and 900, respectively; Form Division 02 has no exact counterpart, the closest being 030

000–007.9 Note that these numbers were included in the schedules because they were needed for works too broad in scope to go elsewhere; they should be used only for such inclusive works

006   *See* **384**

010's **A** Note that some bibliographies are not in tabular form but in paragraphs. In either form they may be annotated or critical. The form does not affect their classification

    B Note that biobibliographies are usually more bibliographic than biographic in purpose, and should, therefore, go in the appropriate subdivisions of 010

010.18   *See* **025.171 A**

010.78   Include here works on the value and methods of using electronic data and other machines in selecting and compiling entries for bibliographies; but class the application of these methods to the compilation of bibliographies in a specific subject in the appropriate subdivision of 016, *e.g.*, bibliographies of chemistry **016.54**

012–015   *See* **016 A**

012   *History*   Before Edition 16 the Office used 012 for all bibliographies of individuals, with appropriate alternative subject bibliography numbers in brackets

See also 016.92

015   A   Include in subdivisions of this number general lists of works in which the place of publication is the determining factor for inclusion, even if the arrangement is by subject

      B   Note that a catalog issued by a firm which is both publisher and bookseller goes in the appropriate subdivision of 015 if limited to its own publications, but in 017.4, 018.4, 019.4 if it includes works issued by other publishers for sale by the bookseller

See also 017–019; 025.171 A

016   A   Note that this number takes precedence over 012–015, 017–019, and includes selected bibliographies, library or auction catalogs, publishers' lists, and all other lists of works on a specific subject

      B   Include here collections of abstracts on a subject when the abstracts are too brief to furnish useful information in themselves

      C   Include here annotated subject bibliographies. Note that annotations characterize books without in themselves supplying information on a subject. Reviews, on the other hand, evaluate books, give substantial indication of their content, and thus deal with their subjects as much as with the books themselves. Class collections of book reviews limited to a specific subject in the number for the subject followed by Form Division 08+, collections not so limited in 028, reviews of a specific book with the book

See also **General Principles** x A, xv; 010.78; 017–019; 025.171 A

016.016   Class here with further subdivision like 016 bibliographies of bibliographies of a subject, *e.g.*, bibliographies of bibliographies of chemistry 016.016 54

016.92   Include in this number and its subdivisions bibliographies of works *about* biography, bibliographies of collected biographies, and bibliographies of individual biographies of several or many persons; but class bibliographies of biographies of one person with bibliographies of works by and about that person, in 012 or the appropriate subject subdivision of 016

017–019   Class here lists of works in a specific library or group of libraries, or of works on sale by a specific bookseller or auctioneer. To go in 017–019, a catalog must list books on a wide variety of subjects (otherwise it would go in an appropriate subdivision of 016), and must list books by many publishers in many places (otherwise it would go in a subdivision of 015). Catalogs of rare books go in 016.09. A catalog of a special library usually is predominantly a list of books in the library's special field and therefore goes in the appropriate subdivision of 016

See also **016 A**

017.4, 018.4, 019.4   *See* **015 B**

021.1   Class here regional library centers that are storage places for seldom wanted material; include in 025.2 centers for cooperative or centralized book acquisition, in 025.26 centers for exchange of duplicates, in 025.35 centers for cooperative or centralized cataloging

025.171 A   Include here comprehensive works on archives, in or out of libraries. Class in 010.18 instructions for making bibliographies, lists, calendars, inventories of archives; in 015+ lists of archives originating in a specific place and not limited by subject; in 016+ lists limited to a specific subject

B *History*   Before Edition 16 the Office used 025.171 instead of 026.973 for the National Archives of the United States

025.2   *See* 021.1

025.26   *See* 021.1

025.35   *See* 021.1

025.7 and 025.84   Include in 025.7 repair of damage to library materials, in 025.84 prevention of damage

026–027   In deciding where to class general works about a specific library, (1) consider whether the contents of the library fall mostly within a specific subject field. If so, class in the appropriate subdivision of 026. If not, (2) consider whether the library is intended for a specific group of users. If so, class in the appropriate number in 027.6–027.8, *e.g.*, libraries for the use of patients in hospitals 027.662, libraries for the use of university students and faculty 027.7. If not, (3) consider the ownership and organization of the library, and class in the appropriate number in 027.1–027.4, *e.g.*, subscription libraries 027.3, family libraries 027.1

026.973   Include in the appropriate subdivision of this number a United States presidential library containing the President's papers together with works on his period and his special interests, *e.g.*, Franklin D. Roosevelt Library 026.973 917

027   *See* 026–027

027.1–027.4   *See* 026–027

027.4   Note that a public library (1) is usually not limited as to clientele within its community except as is necessary for protection of its contents or as is due to limitations of its physical plant, and (2) is usually owned, operated, and financially supported by the government of the area which it serves, and (3) gives most of its services free to residents of that area

027.42   *History*   Before Edition 16 the Office used 027.42 instead of 027.43–027.49 for specific county libraries

027.5   *History*   Before Edition 16 the Office used 027.5 instead of 026.973+ for United States presidential libraries

027.6–027.8   *See* 026–027

028   Include here "book clubs" whose purpose is to promote good reading; in 374.22 those which meet as reading and discussion groups; in 655.58 those which distribute books by mail

    See also 016 C

028.7–028.8   Include here the use of books and libraries without limitation as to kind of library

029.6   *See* 651.7

030–050   *History*   Until *Notes and Decisions* [First Series] no. 2, February 1935, provided subdivision by language, the Office used geographic subdivision similar to that of 071–079

030's   A   Include here picture encyclopedias, and books of wonders and facts that are too inclusive to go with a subject and can be used much like encyclopedias

        B   As with any translation, class a translation of a specific encyclopedia with the original, *e.g.*, English translation of a French encyclopedia 034. *See* **General Principles** XII

040's   A   Include in the 040's collections of short articles which are on such a diversity of subjects that they cannot go with a specific subject, and which are of subject rather than of literary interest. The distinction between the 040's and 081–082 is largely one of length of articles, the 040's being for collections of writings, by one or more authors, which are short, informal, general in treatment; 081–082, for collections of writings which are lengthy, complete, learned or scholarly, specific in treatment. When in doubt, prefer 081–082

B   The distinction between the 040's and the essay numbers in the 800's sometimes requires literary judgments. If the essays are by authors of recognized literary stature, it is safe to class collections in the 800's. *Example:* A collection of editorials by an American journalist known only for his newspaper work goes in 041, but a collection of William Allen White's editorials in 814.52. *See* **General Principles** III

050   Include here, without subdivision, multilingual periodicals

070.3   *See* **650's B**

070.44   Class in subdivisions of 070.44 journalism as applied to departments, columns, sections on specific subjects in general newspapers; in 070.48 journalism as applied to whole journals on specific subjects

070.447   Class here newspaper criticism of motion pictures and radio and television programs; in 070.46 journalism thru the medium of radio, television, and motion pictures

070.46   *See* **070.447**

070.48   Include here journalism for journals having a special kind of audience, *e.g.*, prison journals, journals for "new literates." *See also* **070.44**

081–082   *See* **General Principles** xv; **040's A**

082.2   Class here collections of extracts, usually very short, from larger works, and of briefer pieces of miscellany

091   *See* **417**

099   *See* **General Principles** xv

100 Philosophy

100's vs. 200's   Philosophy deals with the basic realities, such as knowledge, being, conduct, beauty (epistemology, ontology, ethics, esthetics) thru the development of theories and principles based on scientific knowledge or speculation or both; class such works in the 100's. Religion deals with many of the same topics in the context of revelation, deity, worship, salvation; class such works in the 200's. Natural religion or theology lacks the idea of revelation and substitutes for it pure reason; however, its recognition of deity and worship justifies its position in the 210's

112   Note that the phrase "classification of the sciences" is frequently used in the sense of classification of knowledge, and works so called belong here; but classification of the natural sciences goes in 501.2

133.81   Note that this number is limited to *research* on extrasensory perception; general works on this subject go in 133.8

136.7   Class here the principles of child psychology, in 649.1 their application to child care in the home

137.8   *See* **151.2**

140's   Class in the 140's specific philosophical topics or schools; but include in 180–199 collected works of individual philosophers and works about their philosophy. Occasionally the two may overlap, as when the work of one man serves as the foundation of a system or school; in that case, prefer 180–199. But class an individual philosopher's treatise on any specific subject with the subject

150's   Note that psychology, once held to be a branch of philosophy, is now considered both a natural and a social science, and more logically belongs under 500. *See also* **500's**

151.2   Class here tests measuring native intelligence and ability; in **137.8** tests measuring or revealing personality characteristics; in **371.26** tests measuring educational achievement, either the stage attained at a specific time or the advance made within a specific period. Include with each its construction and administration, and interpretation of its results

152.2   *See* **781.15**

164   Note that symbolic logic uses symbols rather than words in developing the reasoning processes. Altho some of the symbols are similar to those used in mathematics, the processes are not specifically mathematical

170's   *History*   Many of the topics in the 170's, such as divorce, temperance, the drug habit, long were considered matters solely of ethics. Even tho the modern approach to these topics is generally sociological, psychological, or medical, it is only in Editions 15 and 16 that the Classification made provision for these more objective aspects. Until then the Office continued to use the numbers in 170 for all aspects, but the subdivisions of 170 are now limited to ethical considerations

171   Class in this number and its subdivisions ethical theories and systems of ethics based on them; but class the ethics of a specific action, situation, condition, or trait in **172–179**. *See also* **172–179**

171.1   Class here the ethical theory that the principles of the highest good are handed down by deity; in **241** (for Christianity) and **291.5** (for comparative religion) rules of conduct based on the appropriate authoritarian theory; in **248.4** (for Christianity) and **291.4** (for comparative religion) applications of these rules to personal living

172–179   Class here ethical principles, theories, systems applied to specific situations and, especially in **179**, specific ethical traits. Class other aspects elsewhere. *Examples:* ethical aspects of liberty of conscience **172.3**, guarantee and pro-

tection by the state of that liberty as an individual right
323.44. *See also* **171**

173   *History*   Before *Notes and Decisions*, Second Series, no.
3, January 1943, authorized **392** for sociology of the family,
the Office used **173**; it then used **392** until Edition 15 relocated the subject to **301.42**

180–199   *See* **140's**

190's   Note that modern Western philosophy may be considered as
beginning approximately 1500 and including the Renais-
sance period. Compare Form Divisions **090 2–090 3**

200 Religion

200's vs. 100's   *See* 100's vs. 200's

200's   Note that "Christianity" may mean: (1) "the Christian church" or the whole body of Christian believers, organized and unorganized, which goes in 261; (2) the religion of Christians based on doctrinal theology, which goes in the 230's; or (3) the state of being a Christian, which goes in the 240's. Some works on "Christianity" are so comprehensive that they fit in none of these numbers; class them in 200–209

206   Include here societies dealing broadly with religion as a whole or with the Christian religion as a whole, but class in 267 and its subdivisions societies of people banded together for Christian work

208   Include here collected works too broad in scope to go with a specific subject elsewhere in the 200's. Note, however, that collected works which are, in effect, comprehensive treatment of a specific denomination belong in the appropriate subdivisions of the 280's. Each collection by such authors as Martin Luther and Rufus M. Jones must be examined to determine whether it deals more with Christianity as a whole (208) or with a denomination, *e.g.*, Society of Friends 289.608

209   Include here the history of Christianity—the beliefs, practices, organizations of religion based on the teachings of Jesus Christ. Class in 270–270.8 the history of the organized Christian church as a whole and in 274–279 that history limited to specific places. Class in 280.9 with appropriate geographic subdivision works dealing with many denominations or sects in a specific place, sect by sect

210's   Note that the topics of natural theology are not dealt with from the point of view of Christianity or of any other specific religion. Class in 220–289 works related to the teachings of Jesus Christ and the Christian church and in the 290's those related to the teachings of other religions

See also **100's vs. 200's**

220–289   *See* **210's**

220's   **A**   Note the use of certain terms and subject headings with the Bible: (1) Class "criticism and interpretation," "introductions" in 220.6; or, if in commentary form (textual order), in 220.7. (2) Class "publication and distribution" in 220.5 if about translating and editing, in 266 if about distribution as a missionary activity. (3) Class "Bible reading," "Bible study" in 220.07 if about how to read and study, in 220.6 if on the value of Bible reading and study

B   Class a specific event in the Bible with the book in which it is related, *e.g.*, Tower of Babel 222.11, unless specific provision is made elsewhere, *e.g.*, baptism of Jesus Christ 232.95. If the event is related in more than one book, class with the book giving fullest account or with the book coming first

See also **220.6**

220.07   *See* **220's A** (3)

220.5   Include here comprehensive selections from the Bible. Class comprehensive selections from a specific part of the Bible with that part, *e.g.*, selections from Acts of Apostles 226.605. Class selections compiled for a specific purpose with the purpose, *e.g.*, selections chosen to show the divine attributes of God 231.4, selections for daily devotions 242.2

See also **220's A** (2)

220.6   Include here "introductions" dealing with explanation, interpretation, value, and use of the Bible; but note that some "introductions" deal also with canon, text, versions, and history of the Bible, and belong in 220 without subdivision

See also **220's A** (1), (3)

220.7   Note that "commentaries" usually deal with the Bible book by book, chapter by chapter, and often even verse by verse. This feature is what chiefly distinguishes 220.7 from 220.6

See also **220's A** (1)

220.9   Note that in this number and its subdivisions go works on Bible times and events. Class works on Bible times but ranging beyond Bible events with the specific subject

222–224, 226–229   Note that, wherever numbers are divided after **0** like 220, two **0**'s must be used for all form divisions except dictionaries and encyclopedias

225   *See* **General Principles x A**

230's   *See* **200's** (2)

231.73   Include here shrines at which miracles occurred, and pilgrimages to them. *Exception:* Class shrines of Mary in 232.931 7

232–232.97   Include in 232–232.8 doctrine and theories concerning Jesus Christ, but class in 232.9 the events of the life of Jesus. *Examples:* the doctrine of the Resurrection 232.5, narration of the event of the Resurrection 232.97

232.2   Note that the meaning of this number is so closely related to the meaning of 232.1 that modern works are likely to include both, so that 232.2 may be little used

232.3   Include here the atonement of Jesus Christ as one means of redemption, but class in 234.3 comprehensive works on the doctrine of redemption

232.4   Note that, since sacrifice is part of atonement, 232.4 may be little used for modern works

232.6   Class here the doctrine of the Second Coming, or Second Advent, of Jesus Christ to earth at the beginning of the millennium; but class in **236.3** comprehensive works on the millennium

232.7 Include here the doctrine that Jesus Christ at some time will pass judgment on men and their deeds, but class in **236.9** the doctrine of the Last Judgment

232.8 Note that here "humanity" is used as the complement to "divinity." Class in **232.9** the human qualities of Jesus Christ's character

232.9 Include in **232.9** and its subdivisions works on seasons or holidays centering around events in the life of Jesus Christ, if accounts of the events are included, *e.g.*, story of the Magi **232.923**. Class in **242.3** meditations, and in **252.6** sermons, for these seasons or holidays; and class in **394.268** the popular observance of holidays, *e.g.*, of Christmas

See also **232.8**

232.931 7 *See* **231.73**

232.957 Class here accounts of the Last Supper as an event in the life of Jesus Christ; class in **265.3** the sacrament, and in **264** the liturgy, of the Lord's Supper. Use **265.3** for comprehensive works

233.4 Class here the doctrine of man's accountability to God for his actions, but in **241** the codes of conduct and virtues for the practice of which Christians are accountable to God

234.3 *See* **232.3**

236.3 *See* **232.6**

236.9 *See* **232.7**

240's *See* **200's** (3)

241 *See* **171.1; 233.4**

242   Include here readings consisting of Bible verses, prayers, brief paragraphs on Christian living, and intended for use in meditation. Class in 248 the application of meditation to personal religion, and the results

See also 252

242.3   *See* 232.9

243   *See* 252

245 A   Include here comprehensive works on words, music, and writers of hymns; class in 783.9 hymn music and singing, and also, in accordance with customary practices in classification of music, texts of hymns which include both words and music

      B   *History*   Note that Edition 14 provided for denominational subdivision with 0 after language subdivision

246–247   Class here the use of art and art objects by the Christian church, including their religious significance and symbolism, their purpose in the church service, the attitude of the church toward ornamentation; but class in the 700's their artistic creation, description, evaluation

248   *See* 242

248.4   *See* 171.1

250's   Class in the 250's the administration and work of the church on a local level—the regular daily work of pastor and parish. In the 260's "church" refers to organized Christianity as a whole or collectively, or, as in 261, to Christianity both organized and unorganized

252   Class sermons by subject (000–999); if there is no specific subject, class by type (252.1–252.9, 242, 243); if there is neither specific subject nor type, class by denomination (252.01–252.09)

252.4   Class here sermons which deal with the practical application of Christian principles to personal and public situations. These are usually collections too general to go elsewhere

252.6   *See* **232.9**

253.5   Include here the principles and applications of psychology used by the pastor in his work with his parishioners

260's   *See* **250's**

261   *See* **200's** (1)

261.7   *See* **322**

262   Note that in 262.12–262.15 classification is by rank of governing leaders, *e.g.*, bishops 262.12; in 262.16–262.19 it is by system or kind of government, *e.g.*, bishops, deacons, etc. in an episcopal government 262.17

262.2   Note that the parish is the local unit of the church but does not necessarily have geographic limits

262.3–262.4 Class in these two numbers the place and function of leaders, parishes, councils, etc., in episcopal and elected types of church government respectively; but class a specific element of the government with the subject, *e.g.*, councils **262.5**

264   *See* **232.957**

264.1–264.9 Unless there are references to the contrary, each subdivision includes: the place of the subject in public worship; how to plan, conduct, or lead that part of public worship; collections to be used in that part of public worship. *Examples:* Include in **264.4** the place of responsive readings, how to lead them, and collections of readings arranged for responsive use in public worship. But in **264.2** include only the place of music in public worship, and how to fit it into harmony with the rest of the service; while classing in 783 collections of sacred music, and how to conduct church music

265.3   *See* **232.957**

266   *See* **220's A** (2)

267   *See* **206**

270, 274–279 *See* **209**

270.1–270.3 Note that, since there were no denominations before 1054, history of the Apostolic Church goes with general church history in 270.1–270.3; comprehensive works, and writings of church fathers, go in 281.1–281.4

280's   A   In classing a denomination or sect which is not specifically provided for in the schedules or index, consider the following principles: (1) Class a new church with the church with which it is most closely connected historically: (a) class a church which is an offshoot of an existing church with the parent church; (b) class a church which is formed by the merging of two or more existing churches with the larger of the merging churches, or with the merging church whose number is the shorter or appears first in the schedules. (2) If a new church has little connection with existing churches class it in **289.9**

        B   Include in **281.5–289** works dealing comprehensively with all or several aspects of a given denomination. Works limited to a specific subject go with the subject even if it is not divided by denomination, *e.g.,* Methodist theology **230.7**, Methodist missions **266.7**, Methodist revivals **269.2**. General history of a denomination may be considered as dealing with various aspects, and belongs in **281.5–289**. *See also* **270.1–270.3**

        C   Include in the subdivisions of these numbers, without further subdivision, those texts upon which certain denominations have been founded or which they consider basic, *e.g.,* *Book of Mormon* **289.3**, *Science and Health* **289.5**. But class texts on a specific subject with the subject, *e.g.,* John Wesley on Christian perfection **234**. *See also* **291.82**

See also **208**

280.9	*See* **209**
281.1–281.4	*See* **270.1–270.3**
282	*See* **General Principles** VII
289.3	*See* **280's C**
289.5	*See* **280's C**
290's	*See* **210's**

291   *History*   For about two years, 1931–1933, the Office used an unprinted expansion of **291** supplied by the editors. *Notes and Decisions* [First Series] no. 1, February 1934, stated that this expansion was being revised by the editors and, therefore, with the exception of **291.37**, was no longer being used

291.4   *See* **171.1**

291.5   *See* **171.1**

291.82 (and **296.1, 297.1** and subdivision **82** in other parts of **292–299**) "Sacred books" are works on which a religion is founded, and are acknowledged by its adherents to be divinely inspired and to constitute religious authority. The original works, therefore, are presumably quite old in the history of the religion's hold upon its adherents. Class here such works (and works about them) even if they are in a recognized literary form such as poetry or drama. But class in the 800's later religious works in a recognized literary form, and with the specific subject those not in a recognized literary form, *e.g.*, doctrinal works by followers of Taoism 299.514 2

See also 280's **C**

296.1 *See* **291.82**

297.1 *See* **291.82**

300 Social Sciences

301   *See* **General Principles** IX **D** (3); **Form Divisions F; 390's**

301.2   Class in this number and its subdivisions comprehensive and theoretical works. Include in 914–919 works limited geographically, and in 309.1 those limited to social conditions as well as limited geographically

301.243 *See* **General Principles** IX **C**

301.32   *See* **312**

301.35   Note that "rural" does not necessarily mean agricultural, but, rather, country environment in contrast to city. This distinction applies also to 323.354

309.1   Note that, as a form division under 300, this number is used for the social sciences as a whole, limited geographically. To be broad enough for 914–919 a work must include more than the subjects of the 300's, *e.g.*, philosophy and religion, language and literature, the arts, treated comprehensively but limited geographically

      See also **301.2; 309.2 A; 342 B**

309.2 **A** Class here what social conditions will be or should be in the future, and how to bring them about; in 309.1 surveys and descriptions of what they are or have been

   B Note that this number is as broad as the 300's. Class here general works on social planning, covering such diverse subjects as the economy, education, social welfare, public administration, communication; class in 338.9 works limited to planning in the economic sphere.

309.22–309.26
   A Note that the order here is from large units to small. "Regions," therefore, are smaller than national areas and larger

than states, *e.g.*, New England; or they may be areas which cut across boundary lines of several states, *e.g.*, Tennessee Valley. "States," like states of the United States, are major political subdivisions of a "national" area. The order of 711.2–711.4 is similar

B   Note that "national," "regional," "state," "city" refer to the unit of planning, *e.g.*, planning for Chicago 309.260 977 311, for many cities in Illinois 309.260 977 3 *not* 309.250 977 3

309.22   Note that the term "technical assistance" as generally used in government publications has a much broader meaning than the words themselves imply. Truly *technical* assistance deals with techniques and procedures of mining, metallurgy, agriculture, etc., and goes in the appropriate subdivisions of 600

309.3–309.9   *History*   Before Edition 16 the Office used 309.3–309.9 instead of 309.1+ for social conditions in specific places

311.2   Class here techniques for collecting statistics and interpreting their meaning. Class in 519.9 sampling and other mathematical methods for determining collection procedures, and mathematical methods of interpretation of the data collected

312   Class here vital statistics themselves and works about them, in 614.1 registration and certification of vital statistics, in 301.32 theories and study of population

312.26   Include here, without subdivision, statistics of deaths due to diseases included in 617–618 but not in 616

312.3   Include here, without subdivision, statistics of the crippled and disabled, and of the incidence of diseases included in 617–618 but not in 616

312.8   Include here statistics of increase and decrease of population

320's   Class in 320.1 and 321 *general* theories and principles of
             government, and descriptions of the various forms of state,
             e.g., theory of the federal state 321.021; but class their ap-
             plication to a specific government or constitution in 342,
             e.g., application of the federal form of state in the United
             States Constitution 342.73; class their application to the
             executive branch in the 350's (with general works in 351–
             352 and specific applications in 352.03–352.09, 353–354);
             class both general and specific applications to the legislative
             branch in 328, both general and specific applications to the
             judicial branch in 347.9. Class in 322–329 *specific* theories
             and principles, and their application to specific govern-
             ments

             See also **909, 930–999**

321   Note that 321.01–321.07 divides forms of state by scope and
             extent of responsibility and sovereignty, while 321.1–321.9
             divides them by the base upon which power or sovereignty
             is founded

321.4   Important examples of pure democracy are the government
             of ancient Athens, and local government of New England
             thru town meetings

321.642   *See* **335.43**

321.8   *See* **General Principles** VII

322   Class here theories of the relationship of the state to the
             church, or organized body of religion; but class in 261.7 the
             duties and obligations of the Christian church toward po-
             litical problems, *e.g.*, freedom of speech

323.1–323.3 *History*   Before Edition 15 the Office used 323.1–323.3
             instead of 301.3–301.4 for the sociological aspects of ethnic
             groups, minorities, social classes, communities

323.2   *See* **335.43**

323.354   *See* **301.35**

323.44   *See* **172–179**

323.65–323.67   *See* **342 B**

323.673   *See* **327**

324.23   Include here the principles and theory of party conventions, but in 329 plans for and accounts of actual conventions

325   Note that, when limited geographically, the subjects of 325.1 go in 325.4–325.9, those of 325.2–325.21 in 325.23–325.29, and those of 325.3–325.31 in 325.33–325.39. These are exceptions to the general principle that classification by most specific subject takes precedence over place. *See also* **General Principles** iv

325.21 and 325.31   *History*   Note that each of these has been narrowed to the scope of one of its Edition 14 subdivisions, topics in the other subdivisions going back to 325.2 and 325.3 respectively

325.21   Include here promotion and assistance in emigrating from a country, but class in 361.53 general care and aid to refugees

325.23–325.29   Include here emigration laws; however, most codes include both immigration and emigration laws, and go in 325.4–325.9

325.31   *See* **325.21 and 325.31**

327   Include here international relations which are broader than diplomatic relations but to some extent based upon them. The Library of Congress subject heading usually includes "relations (general)." Class purely cultural relations and

relations limited to a specific subject with the subject, *e.g.,* passports 323.673

See also 974–979

327.3–327.9   Note that Edition 16 has changed the notation for the second geographic subdivision by dropping "9" from the "09" and "009" of Edition 14, *e.g.,* foreign relations between England and France 327.420 44

328   Note that specific subdivisions are provided under each country in 328.4–328.9 for rules and legislative manuals. These are exceptions to the general principle that classification by most specific subject takes precedence over place. *See also* **General Principles** IV

See also **320's**

328.37   *See* **General Principles** XIII

328.4–328.9

A   Include here with each legislature its calendar of bills of the session and records of bills considered, but class in 345, 346, 349 the collected bills after they have become session laws

B   Class in the subdivisions 02–04 under the numbers for specific countries general collections of legislative debates, abstracts, documents; but class those on a specific subject with the subject

C   Include here works limited to only one house of bicameral legislative bodies, *e.g.,* rules of the United States Senate 328.735

329   *See* 324.23

329.01   Class here campaign books, pamphlets, broadsides, issued by one or more parties before election day, to influence votes. Class in 973 works about a specific campaign, *e.g.*, history of the 1960 Kennedy-Nixon campaign 973.921. Before Edition 16 the Office used 329.01 for works about specific campaigns

329.8–329.9   *See* 335.43

330.18–330.19   *See* **General Principles** x **B**

330.9   *See* **General Principles** x **A**

330.973   *See* 909, 930–999; 914–919 **A**

331   *In order to understand fully all the statements that follow on 331 and its subdivisions, refer not only to Edition 16 but also to* Decimal Classification Additions, Notes, and Decisions, *v. 1, no. 10/11*

331   **A**   Class in 331 and its subdivisions the theories and principles of labor and the laboring classes as factors in the economy, in 658.3 and its subdivisions the application of these theories and principles to personnel management; class comprehensive works on both in 331. In the broad sense used here the laboring classes include all persons who engage in physical or mental toil for personal gain or economic production

      B   Class specific labor aspects of specific occupations and enterprises in the appropriate subdivisions of 331, dividing by occupation or enterprise when the schedules so provide, *e.g.*, unemployment in mining industry 331.137 822, government intervention in airline labor disputes 331.898. Note that cross references under certain labor aspects make exception of public service employment, both civil and military, *e.g.*, labor-management relations of central government employees 351.17 *not* 331.181 35, tenure of office of central government employees 351.4 *not* 331.117. But note also that 331.795 is specifically provided for comprehensive works on the economics of public service

      History   *See* **656**

331.11 and 331.13   *See* **General Principles** IX **A** (1) (b) 1

331.137 8   *See* **General Principles** IX **A** (2) 1

331.155   *See* **380.12**

331.252   Class here pension systems set up by management or labor or both, and supported by management or both, under which pensions are paid by employer to employees retired because of age or disablement; but class in **368.4** social security programs sponsored by the government, under which provision is made for insurance against accident, illness, unemployment, as well as for payment of retirement benefits

331.28   *See* **General Principles** IX **A** (2) 1, XXI (3)

331.282 13   *See* **General Principles** IX **B**

331.3–331.6   Unless there is specific emphasis, class overlapping groups with the group coming first in the schedules, *e.g.*, work by physically disabled Negro women **331.4**

331.51   Class here convict labor as a factor in the economy; but class in **365.65** the planning and administration of convict labor, and its value in penology. Use **331.51** for comprehensive works

331.7   Include here alphabetic and classified lists of occupations other than those prepared for vocational guidance use, which go in **371.425**

See also **General Principles** IX **A** (2) 1

331.762 13   *See* **General Principles** IX **B**

331.795   *See* **331 B**

331.818   *See* **General Principles** IX **A** (2) 1

331.825   Include here theoretical works on labor's right to protection; but class in 368.41 administration and implementation

331.833   Class here the effects of housing on the health and welfare of laboring classes, but in 711.58–711.59 the design of housing areas to achieve these effects. Use 331.833 for comprehensive works

         See also **General Principles** ix **A** (1) (a) 1

331.898   *See* **331 B**

332.024   *See* **332.14**

332.1–332.3   Class histories or reports of a specific bank in the appropriate number followed where applicable by Form Division 09+ *not* 065

         See also **650's B**

332.14   Include here financial management of property and estates by personal or corporate trustees; include in 332.024 management of one's personal finances, in 336.24 financial management of property and estates to minimize income taxes, in 347.65 the management of decedent estates in conformity with a testator's will

332.2   *See* **339.43**

332.45   Class here works on "sterling area," "hard currency area," and the like only if the subject is foreign exchange; class such works with other specific subjects when required, *e.g.*, foreign trade 382

332.67   Include here evaluation of specific stocks and bonds as investments

332.673   Class here foreign investments as financial transactions, but include in 338.91 foreign investments as a factor in economic assistance

332.678   *See* **339.43**

332.71–332.72   Include in 332.71 loans on crops and livestock, in 332.72 loans on farm land

333.33   *See* **650's B**

333.332–333.38   Note that 333.34–333.38 take precedence over 333.335–333.339, *e.g.*, subdivision of urban real estate 333.38; but that 333.335–333.339 take precedence over 333.332–333.334, *e.g.*, appraisal of urban real estate 333.337

333.332   Include here the effect on real estate values of such factors as highways, airports, schools, churches, factories

333.910 975 2   *See* **General Principles** XIV

334.683   Note that the "collective farms" of communist countries are government owned or controlled, and go in **338.12**

335   Note that the order of the subdivisions is largely historical, and that the geographic adjectives indicate kinds of socialism by country of origin, *e.g.*, English utopian socialism in United States 335.120 973, modern English socialism **335.509 42**

335.01   *History*   Before Edition 16 the Office used 335.01 instead of 330.17 for comprehensive works on theory of property

335.43   Class here communism as an economic system, and comprehensive works on communism; in **321.642** theory and principles of communism as a form of government; in **323.2** subversive activities by communists; in **329.8–329.9** communist parties; in **338** economic production in communist countries; in **342.4–342.9** constitutional law and history of communist nations; in **352** and **354** their administrative government; in **940–999** the history of events leading to the establishment of communism in a specific nation, and a history of that nation under communism. Observe similar distinctions in classing works on fascism

336   Note that 336.1–336.34 deal with *incoming* funds, and 336.36–336.39 with *outgoing* funds. In accordance with the general principle that classification is by most specific subject and only then by place, class in 336.4–336.9 only works dealing with a variety of topics on public finance in a specific place. *See* **General Principles** IV

336.24   *See* **332.14**

336.266   *See* **337.5**

336.34   Class in 336.343 3 the debt owed by a government to its own citizens, how much it is, and why; class in 336.343 5 its debt to foreign governments and citizens. Use 336.343 3 for comprehensive works

336.36–336.39   *See* **336**

336.39   Note that most works on the spending of a specific government deal also with its income, and therefore go in 336.4–336.9. Most works in 336.39 deal with theory of government spending, its justification, its relationship to private spending, its effect on the economy, and similar topics

336.4–336.9   *See* **336; 336.39; 351.72**

337.5   Include here "escape-clause" publications of the Tariff Commission, and other works the purpose of which is to modify tariff duties in relation to protection of specific domestic industries. Class in appropriate subdivisions of 338.1–338.4 works emphasizing the economic status of specific industries. Class in 336.266 schedules of duties on specific commodities as a source of revenue

338   A   Class in 338 and its subdivisions comprehensive works on both the economic and technical aspects of industry and production. Specific examples appear in some of the notes following, *e.g.*, 338.1

B   Include here (or in 338.012 if classified) general lists of
commodities or commercial products; include in subdivisions of 338.1–338.4 general lists of specific products or
groups of products; class lists arranged or annotated for a
specific purpose with the purpose, *e.g.*, lists for use in export 382.6

See also **General Principles** IX **D** (3); **335.43**

338.058   Class here directories of buyers and sellers, exporters and
importers of various enumerated primary and secondary
commodities or commercial products; include in subdivisions of 338.1–338.4 directories of dealers in specific products or groups of products, *e.g.*, of agricultural products
generally 338.140 58, of raw cotton 338.173 51, of cotton
textiles 338.476 772 1. Class in the 600's directories of producers of such products, *e.g.*, of various primary and secondary products 605.8, of agricultural products 630.58, of
raw cotton 633.510 58, of cotton textiles 677.210 58. Class
directories of both dealers and producers in 338+

338.1–338.4   Class here comprehensive works on the economic aspects
of specific industries and firms; class in 338.6 the economic
aspects of various productive systems or methods; class in
338.7–338.8 the economic aspects of the integration and
management structure of the organizations or firms within
various industries, and in 338.76 such structure by industry; class in 658 the technique of industrial management;
class in the 600's, or elsewhere by subject, techniques and
processes. Class works dealing with both economic and
technical aspects of an industry in 338.1–338.4. Class house
organs in 338+ or 600's as appropriate, followed where applicable by Form Division 065

See also **337.5; 338 B; 338.058**

338.1   Class in 338.1 and its subdivisions the economic aspects of
agricultural production, *e.g.*, prices, marketing, statistics,
crop reports, place of agriculture in the economy; class in

the 630's the technical aspects of agricultural production; use 338.1 for comprehensive works. Similarly class works on international agricultural assistance, dividing specific numbers geographically by countries receiving such assistance

338.109   Include in 338.109+ agricultural products in general. Limit 338.19+ to *food* supply, including there without geographic subdivision comprehensive works not emphasizing maladjustments

338.12   *History*   Note that Edition 16 narrows the meaning of this number from that in Edition 14, dropping some topics back to 338.1

    See also **334.683**

338.14   Class economic aspects of grading and inspecting agricultural products in 338.14 (and 338.17 for specific products), technical aspects in 631.56 (and 633–639 for specific products), public health aspects in 614.3. Include in 658.896 3 grading and inspecting as a part of direct farm marketing

338.140 58   *See* **338.058**

338.17   Class in the subdivisions of 338.17, 338.27, 338.37 the economic aspects of specific raw products grown in or on or extracted from the earth, and in the subdivisions of 338.47 the economic aspects of intermediate products or completed products converted from raw products. *Examples:* Economic aspects of raising sugar cane 338.173 61, of manufacture of cane sugar 338.476 641 22; of extracting petroleum 338.272 82, of refined gasolines 338.476 655 382. Class comprehensive works on both the raw and the manufactured product with the raw product

    See also **338.14**

338.173 51   *See* **338.058**

338.179 1   *History*   Before Edition 15 the Office used **338.179 1** instead of **338.372** for hunting industries

338.19   *See* **338.109**

338.2   *See* **553**

338.27   *See* **338.17**

338.3   *History*   Before Edition 15 the Office used this for water products only

338.37   *See* **338.17**

338.45   *See* **General Principles** ɪx **C**

338.456   Class here the economic effects of the use of machinery in specific industries, but in **338.47** the economic aspects of the manufacture of that machinery, *e.g.*, economic effects of use of machinery in agriculture **338.456 3**, economic aspects of the manufacture of agricultural machinery **338.476 817 63**

338.47   *See* **338.17**; **338.456**

338.476 772 1   *See* **338.058**

338.476 817 63   *See* **338.456**

338.6   *History*   Note that headings and notes in Edition 16 narrow the meanings somewhat from those in Edition 14

       See also **338.1–338.4**

338.64   Include here industries in which labor is by the skilled trades, with work largely hand-done with hand tools and small hand-operated even tho power-driven machines, where designs and patterns vary from product to product as result of human variations

338.65   Include here industries using heavy machines tended by unskilled labor, where the use of dies and templates results in products being made up of interchangeable parts

338.7–338.8   *See* **338.1–338.4; 658.1 B**

338.9   *See* **309.2 B**

338.91   *History*   Before Edition 16 provided that this number be limited to international planning, *i.e.*, of one country for another or of two or more together, the Office used it for industrial planning, planned economy, and similar topics. These works now go in **338.9**. Country subdivision continues to be in **338.93–338.99**

                  See also **332.673**

339.4   Note that national resources include, in addition to natural resources (the resources in the natural world), those which result from man's activities, *e.g.*, money, railroads, housing, manufactures; also, labor, or human resources, with the training, experience, and natural skill thereof

339.43   Class here the broad social and economic aspects and consequences of saving, either personal or corporate; class in **332.678** procedures of investment; in **332.2** procedures and mechanics of saving, both in banks and at home

341.13   *See* **General Principles** IV

341.18   Class here organizations general in character but formed to deal with problems in specific regions, even tho countries outside the region are included in the membership. Use geographic subdivision for the region covered. *Example:* SEATO **341.185 9**

341.3   Include here rules and conventions adopted by nations to minimize war's brutality; but in **355** the theory, principles, and conduct of warfare

342 **A** Class here the application of the provisions of a constitution to all three branches of a government—legislative, executive, and judicial. Class in 353–354 works limited to the
executive or administrative branch, also works on the rela-
tionships among the three branches when limited to practical administrative considerations. Other things being
equal, the presence of the text of the constitution with references to it from the text of the work tends to tip the scales
in favor of 342

B Include here or in 353–354 works on "civics" which deal
with the structure and operations of the government, in
323.65 or 323.67 those dealing with the duties and privileges
of citizens, and in 309.1 those dealing broadly with social
affairs, services and conditions in a country

See also **320's**

342.4–342.9 *See* **335.43**

342.74–342.79, 342.969 Note that works on the government of a specific state of the United States often contain sections on the
United States Federal government; unless the latter is emphasized, class in 342.74–342.79, 342.969

345–346, 349 Class "citations" and "annotations" with the works to
which the citations or annotations are made, *e.g.*, to state
law reports 345.42

See also **328.4–328.9 A**

345.1–345.5 The following definitions may provide helpful distinctions:
Session laws are the laws enacted at each session of the legislative body, printed in full in the order of enactment.
Statutes at large are all the laws, printed in full in the order
of enactment. *Codes* or *revised statutes*, also known as *compiled statutes*, are bodies of laws collected, revised, and
arranged in systematic order by subject. *Law digests* consist of quotations, paraphrases, abridgments, but do not
give full texts. *Reports* give full accounts of cases argued

before and decisions rendered by the courts, and are usually official publications. *Digests of cases* give summarized accounts of cases argued before and decisions rendered by the courts, and are usually unofficial publications

347   Class here that branch of law which is neither international, constitutional, nor criminal, but which deals with the relations of individuals to each other

347 Form Divisions *History*   Before Edition 16 provided specifically for the use of two-0 numbers as required for form divisions under 340 the Office used 347, *e.g.*, before Edition 16 bar associations were 347.062 instead of 340.062

347.42   Class here the legal aspects of sales as contracts, with their possibilities for damage if not fulfilled; but class in **658.8** and its subdivisions the history, description, and techniques of selling

347.65   *See* **332.14**

347.9   *See* **320's**

348   Include here those topics in canon law which in secular law would go in 342, 343, 345, 346, 347, 349, *e.g.*, procedure, courts; but class canon law of other subjects with the subject, *e.g.*, canon law on censorship 323.402 6

349   *See* **328.4–328.9 A; 345–346, 349**

350–354   Class principles and theories of public administration of central governments in **351** and its subdivisions, of local governments in 352–352.008, 352.1–352.9, of both together in **350**. Class the application of *general* principles and theories to specific local governments in 352.03–352.09, and their application to the executive branches of specific central governments in 353–354. Include also in 351.1–351.9 and 352.1–352.9, with appropriate geographic subdivision, the application of these *specific* topics to specific central governments and specific local governments respectively

See also **320's**

351–352   *See* **658.3**

351   *See* **350–354**

351.1–351.6   Include in 351.1–351.2 comprehensive works only. Class these subjects in relation to specific offices, bureaus, agencies and the like with the office, bureau, or agency, *e.g.*, selection of United States postal employees 383.497 3. But include in 351.3–351.6 these subjects in relation to civil service employees and employment no matter what the specific occupation, activity, or service

351.1   Note that most modern works on the "merit system" in civil service deal with the employment, promotion, and organization of civil service employees on the basis of their fitness for their jobs. Class such works in 351.1 and its subdivisions. But class in 351.6 works dealing with the merit system versus the spoils system

351.17   *See* **331 B**

351.3   Note that, contrary to the general principle of classification by most specific subject, civil service examinations are kept together, because (1) the chief interest in them is as avenues for securing civil service jobs, often, at the lower levels, without much regard to subject specialization in the jobs, and (2) almost all of the examinations include general information questions applicable to any position. Use 351.3 without subdivision for those examinations which have no reasonable basis for the "divide like" provision. Examinations other than civil service go with the subject, using Form Division 076. *See also* **General Principles** **IV**

351.4   *See* **331 B**

351.6   *See* **351.1**

351.711   *See* **355.62**

351.72   Class here the making of government budgets—theory, principles, techniques; but class the budget itself (the projected total financial picture of receipts and expenditures) of the whole government in 336.4–336.9, of a part of the government with the part

352   *See* **Form Divisions C; 335.43; 350–354**

352.03–352.09   Since communes, like United States counties, are units of local government or administration, class here their organization and management, in 914–919 the life and activities of the areas governed by them

353–354 A Class in subdivisions of these numbers comprehensive works on specific major government departments; but, in accordance with the cross references under 353.09 and 353.1–353.8, class independent and subordinate agencies with their respective subjects, using Form Division 061

B   Class here works dealing about equally with the central and local governments of a country or state, *e.g.*, the central administrative government of Massachusetts and the local governments of Massachusetts 353.974 4

See also **342 A; 350–354**

353.09   *See* **353–354 A**

353.1–353.8 Class here works on a department as a whole, *e.g.*, organization or reorganization, history, hearings on appropriation bills and nominations for top policy-making positions. Note that these numbers, with the exception of 353.7, are for departments whose heads are cabinet members

See also **General Principles** XIII; **353–354 A**

353.1   *See* **General Principles** XIV

353.6   *See* **355 B**

354   *See* **335.43; 350–354; 355 B**

355–359 A Note that any activity of the armed forces may have several aspects: (1) class in **355.34** and **356–358** units organized for the activity; (2) class in **355.6** administration of the activity; (3) class in **355.7** installations needed for the activity; (4) class in **355.8** equipment needed; (5) class with the subject, usually in the **600**'s, technical methods; (6) class comprehensive works with the organizational unit

B   Class in **355–359** these topics as applied to many wars or to no specific war, but class in the **900**'s a topic limited to one war, *e.g.*, strategy in World War II **940.540 1**. Class military history of a specific country with history of that country

See also **355.61–355.63; 623 A; 658.3**

355 A   Include here general military missions and military assistance from one country to another, with geographic subdivision for the country to which the mission or assistance is sent. Class missions or assistance relating to a specific subject with the subject, *e.g.*, loan of submarines **359.32**

B   Include here hearings on appropriation bills which are limited to the armed forces, but in **353.6** or the appropriate subdivision of **354** those pertaining to the entire department of defense including nonmilitary activities

See also **341.3; 355.45**

355.02   Be careful to class here only general handbooks and outlines of military science. Most officers' handbooks deal with specific subjects or with specific services

355.07   Note that two aspects of the education and training of members of the armed forces have both military and nonmilitary aims: physical training or athletics, and nonmilitary education. Class both in the appropriate general numbers, *e.g.*, adult education 374, but class in 355.34 the units or corps of the armed forces which arrange for and administer these forms of education

355.076   *See* 355.223

355.09   Class here the history of military science and of methods of warfare; but class in the 900's with the general political history of the countries involved the history of a specific war or wars. Limit 355.48 to technical analyses of military events as illustrating tactics and strategy

355.223   Include here examinations intended to determine the acceptance and placement of recruits, but class in 355.076 examinations on military subjects

355.27   Include here the value in time of war of existing peacetime systems of transportation, in 355.41 plans and strategy for transportation of troops and supplies, in 355.83 description and military use of transportation equipment, in 358.25 the organization and work of military units in transportation services, in 623.6 engineering aspects of military transportation

355.34   *See* 355–359 A; 355.07

355.41   *See* 355.27

355.45   Class here "national defense" in the narrow tactical and strategic sense, but in 355 "national defense" in the broad sense of all military plans and policies

355.48   *See* 355.09; 909, 930–999

355.6   *See* 355–359 A

355.61–355.63   Class here comprehensive works; but class in 355.64–355.69 these operations when applied to specific administrative departments, and class in 355–359 with the unit these operations when applied to specific branches of the service, *e.g.*, inspection of chemical warfare services 358.34

355.62   Include here contracts dealing with purely military supplies and matériel; class in 351.711 contracts not limited to such supplies and matériel

355.64–355.8   In cases of doubt give preference to 355.7–355.8 over 355.64–355.69, *e.g.*, lodging administration 355.71, food administration 355.81

355.64–355.69   *See* 355.61–355.63

355.7–355.8   *See* 355–359 A

355.83   *See* 355.27

356–358   *See* 355–359 A

358.25   *See* 355.27

358.4   Note that this includes air services of and air warfare by the army and navy as well as services of and warfare by the air forces

360's   Note that 363, 366, 367, 369 provide specific numbers for certain kinds of societies and that Form Division 06 need not be used with them. For basis of geographic subdivision under these numbers follow the instructions under **Form Divisions 062 3–062 9 A**

361–362   Note that social work and welfare services are not necessarily charity. Altho the activities under 361 and 362.5 are largely charitable, 362.1–362.4, 362.6–362.8 include services that are paid for by their recipients as well as services that are free

361.506   Since the Red Cross is both international and national, both governmental and private, do not subdivide like Form Di-

vision 06. For other organizations for disaster relief use
361.506 and subdivide as appropriate

361.53   *See* **325.21**

362   *See* **361–362**

362.1–362.7   Note that 362.6–362.7 take precedence over 362.1–362.18,
362.2–362.43 but that 362.19 takes precedence over 362.6–
362.7

362.1   *History*   Before Edition 15 the Office used 362.1 instead
of 368.38 for group hospitalization

362.7   *History*   Before Edition 15 the Office used 362.7 instead
of 301.43 for the sociology of youth

363   *See* **360's**

365.65   *See* **331.51**

366–367   *See* **360's**

368   *See* **650's B**

368.4   *See* **331.252**

368.41–368.42   Class in 368.41 insurance against accidents and illness
caused by the conditions of one's employment, and in 368.42
insurance against illness not caused by the job

368.41   *See* **331.825**

368.42   *See* **614.2**

368.44   Include here unemployment statistics based upon analysis
of unemployment claims and intended for use in the study
of claims

369   *See* **360's**

370's   *See* **355.07**

370.1   *See* **375.88**

370.7   *See* **371.11–371.134 A**

370.9   Include here specific schools which comprise all levels from elementary to graduate, but class specific schools of specific levels in 372.9, 373.3–373.9, 378.4–378.98

                  See also **379.4–379.9**

371.11–371.134
    A   Class in 371.11 personal qualifications required of teaching staff, *e.g.*, health; class in 371.12 training and education required (but the training itself in 370.7); class in 371.13 and its subdivisions formal requirements

    B   Note that requirements for teachers of specific subjects go in these numbers; but class the technique or methods of teaching a specific subject at the elementary level in 372.3–372.8, at all other levels with the subject

371.147   Note that in 371.147 goes the organization of the teaching and administrative staff, while in 371.2 go organization and administration of the whole school

371.25–371.26   Include in 371.25 grading of students in the sense of assigning them to appropriate levels, but in 371.26 grading in the sense of evaluating individual accomplishments

371.26   *See* **151.2**

371.27   Class here kinds, value, methods of construction and use of examinations and how to take them successfully. Include also texts of examinations when subjects covered are too broad to go with specific subjects

371.425   *See* **331.7**

371.74–371.75   Include here the place of athletics and games in the school program and in maintenance of health in schools; but class in the appropriate subdivisions of **796** sports and games comprehensively treated

372.3–372.8

    A   Class here works which are designated as *textbooks* for an elementary grade or grades, and works in which the teaching features are so dominant that the works are contributions to how to teach the subject in elementary schools. Otherwise class with the subject

    B   Note that many sets of books on the teaching of a specific subject begin with the elementary grades and continue into junior or even senior high school. Include these in 372.3–372.8 unless the emphasis is distinctly on the higher level, in which case class with the subject. When in doubt, prefer the subject

    See also **371.11–371.134 B**

372.9   *See* **Form Divisions E, F; 370.9**

373.3–373.9   *See* **Form Divisions E, F; 370.9**

374.22   *See* **028**

374.8   Include here those "folk high schools" and "people's colleges" which are really continuation schools and not limited to high school or college level, in 378.15 evening colleges and colleges giving evening courses for academic credit

374.9   *History*   Before Edition 16 the Office used 374.9+ instead of 374.8+ for specific "folk high schools" and continuation schools

375.88   Include here the place of classical literature in the curriculum, but include in 370.1 the broader topic of "classical education"

378 *See* 379.16

378.013 Include here the aims and value of higher education

378.15 *See* 374.8

378.4–378.98 *See* 370.9

379.16 Class here comparisons and contrasts of tax-supported and privately supported colleges and universities, but in 378 general works on higher education both public and private

379.4–379.9 Note that 379.4–379.9 is limited to *public* education in specific places, while 370.9 covers education in general in specific places. When in doubt, prefer 370.9

380's A Note that, altho the heading for this Division was "Commerce Communication" in Edition 14, "Commerce" in Edition 15, and "Public services; public utilities" in Edition 16, the essential coverage remains the same, both for the whole and for the parts

B Class here the business and management aspects of public services; in the 600's their engineering and technical aspects. Use the 380's for comprehensive works on both

See also 650's **B**

380.12 Class here commercial arbitration dealing with disputes arising out of contracts and other transactions between business organizations; but class in 331.155 industrial arbitration dealing with disputes between labor and management

381–382 Note that, contrary to the general principles of classification, comprehensive works on internal and international commerce go in the second of the two numbers. *See also* **General Principles** IX **D** (3)

382 *See* 332.45

382.09   *See* 382.5–382.6

382.5–382.6 Class trade *from* one country *to* another, without apparent emphasis, in the number which reflects the author's nationality, *e.g.*, British exports to France by a Briton 382.609 42, by a Frenchman 382.509 44; if the trade goes both ways, class in 382.09 with geographic division for both countries

382.6   *See* 338 **B**

383.2   Note that most works on stamps, postal cards, and covers are written from the philatelic point of view and go in 383.22

384   Include here comprehensive works on communication between men, in 006 even more comprehensive works on communication and control among machines and animals as well as men

385–388 A Class here the services, business, and management of carrying passengers and hauling commodities—the running of trains, ships, planes, and cars in the sense of providing and maintaining schedules and routes, collecting fares, and the like; also the certification and chartering of businesses carrying on transportation services, their regulation as public utilities, and the training and certification of personnel who maintain the services. Class in the 620's the engineering and mechanical aspects of transportation—the running of trains, ships, planes, and cars, in the sense of their design, construction, maintenance, and efficient use; also the inspection and certification of transport equipment to ensure satisfactory usability, and the training and certification of personnel to take care of the engineering and mechanical aspects. Class comprehensive works on both in 385–388

B   Note that Form Division 065 is used for firms providing transportation, *e.g.*, American Airlines, Inc.; but that Form Division 09 is used for history and local treatment of the service provided, *e.g.*, the air transport services of American

Airlines. Because such services may connect different geographic areas, divide 09 by country only, using the homeland of firms providing international services, *e.g.,* services of Pan American World Airways 387.709 73

See also **711.7**

385.2–385.3 Class in **385.3** only stationary facilities, in **385.2** rolling stock. Class engineering aspects in **625.18** and **625.2** respectively

386.47–386.48 Class in **386.47** canals large enough for seagoing or lake ships, in **386.48** canals for smaller boats and those with shallow draught

386.8, 387.1 Note that it is geographic location, not kind of ships accommodated, that distinguishes seaports from inland ports. A seaport lies directly on ocean, bay, gulf, or sea, or on a river mouth or estuary opening directly on the ocean, *e.g.,* port of New York **387.129 747 1**, port of New Orleans **386.809 763 355**. Include in both numbers such port facilities as docks, quays, fueling stations, storage facilities

387.11 Note that regulations for a specific port go with the port in **387.129+**

389.1 Class here weights and measures used in commerce and daily life, in **530.8** weights and dimensions in a theoretic sense and their applicability to physics

390's Class here descriptions, histories, comparative works on customs; class in corresponding numbers in **301** the significance of customs and their effects on society, and also comprehensive works

392 *History*   *See* **173**

394   Limit this number and its subdivisions to origin, history, description of customs. *Examples:* pageantry customs 394.5, how to plan and stage a pageant 791.6; history and description of traditional English coronation ceremonies 394.4, account of coronation of Elizabeth II 942.085. But note that 394.268 includes plans, programs, decorations for celebration of specific holidays. *See also* 232.9

395.1   Include here rules of conduct for children on public or social occasions; class in 649.6 training of children to observe such rules

396   Note that the topics in this number and its subdivisions are much broader in scope than the "customs and folklore" named in the heading of 390. This is an exception to **General Principles v A (1)**

398   *See* **800's B**

399   Include here ancient and medieval customs of warfare, also description and use of early arms and armor

400 Language

400's   A   Note that works on the language of a specific subject go in the number for the subject followed by Form Division 014 or 03. *See* **Form Division 014**

      B   Class examples and collections of "texts" the purpose of which is to display and study a language with the language, even if limited to a specific subject

      C   Class in the 400's series of "studies" which emphasize linguistics and literature, even tho they include occasional papers on culture and history; but class in the 900's studies in history and culture which include but do not emphasize linguistics and literature

401.8   Include here history and theory of oral communication between men and its part in the development of civilization and society; in **808.5** the art or technique of oral expression, including choice of words, rhythm and emphasis, tone and pitch, inflection and gesture

411   Include here the history of letters and other symbols used to express sounds which are put together to form words, *i.e.*, alphabets; and of symbols used to express ideas, *e.g.*, Chinese ideographs. Class in **652** practical methods of recording these symbols by hand or machine

417   Include here ancient and medieval handwriting and their variations, and the history of writing in ancient and medieval times; class in **091** ancient and medieval manuscripts, and in **913** archeological excavations of ancient inscriptions

420's   Note that the following observations on **420–428** apply also to those other languages in **429–499** which are divided like 420. *See also* **429–499**

420.7   Class here the "teaching of English" when it includes the history of the language, alphabet, grammar, and the like, *i.e.,* all or most of the subdivisions of 420; class in **428** text-books for learning the fundamentals of practical use of the language; class in **808** the application of these fundamentals to written and oral communication for the achievement of clarity and esthetic pleasure. When in doubt as to choice between **428** and **808**, prefer **808**

421.5   Include here speech training in the sense of pronunciation of words, in **784.93** speech training in the sense of pronunciation in singing, in **808.52** speech training for conversation and public speaking, also comprehensive works on speech training

425   *See* **428.2**

426   Class here the mechanics of writing poetry—rhythm, rhyme, feet, accent; in **808.1** the application of these to the poetic expression of ideas

427   Include here works in dialect the purpose of which is the study of the dialect, but class in the **800**'s those intended to be read as literature. When in doubt, prefer the **800**'s

427.09   Include here slang, whether or not in a dialect, *e.g.,* American slang **427.09**

427.1–427.9   Do not subdivide like **420** a dialect number formed by means of geographic division

427.9   Class here nonliterary forms of the English language outside of England, but class thruout the **420**'s the English language as the standard or literary language used in those countries

428   *See* **420.7**

428.2   Class here "lessons" and other works to be used in learning English, including its grammar; class in **425** historical and expository works on English grammar

428.24   Include here works intended for the use of children, adults, or both

428.4   Include here improvement of good as well as of poor readers in reading speed and comprehension, *e.g.,* "rapid reading" courses

429–499   Note that each language with its own specific number or series of numbers, *e.g.,* Arabic **492.7**, is divided like **420**; but that more than one language in a single number, *e.g.,* Ethiopic **492.8**, is not so divided. *See also* **420's**

500 Pure Science

500's   Pure science is essentially factual and impersonal, dealing with the description, composition, actions and reactions of natural phenomena, both animate and inanimate, and with the development of laws or theories to explain them. The application of scientific facts to human advantage goes with the application, often in the 600's, as technology or applied science. Note that not all pure science is included in the 500's, *e.g.*, 150, 611–612, 781.1; not everything in the 500's is pure science, *e.g.*, parts of 527, of 529, of 578; not all applications of science are in the 600's, *e.g.*, parts of 720, 750, 770; and comprehensive works on applications of specific scientific facts may include such a variety of applications that they go with the scientific facts which are applied, *e.g.*, 537.8

See also **General Principles** ɪx **D** (3); **600's vs. 700's; 630's**

500–509   *See* **Form Divisions D**

501.2   *See* 112

508.3–508.9   *See* 579.6

510's   *See* **Form Divisions E**

510.76   *See* 793.74–793.8

510.78   *See* **Form Divisions D**

519.9   *See* 311.2

525.69   *History*   Before Edition 15 the Office used 525.69 instead of 623.894 for tide tables as aids to navigation

527   *History*   Before Edition 15 the Office used 527 instead of 623.89 for practical sea navigation

See also **500's**

529   *See* 500's

529.43   Include here present-day almanacs based on the Gregorian calendar

530–559   Class a specific property of a specific substance with the property, not with the substance, *e.g.*, electrochemistry of copper compounds 541.37 *not* 546.652 or 549.2 or 553.43, expansion of mercury 536.413 *not* 546.663. But class the application of a specific property with the application, *e.g.*, application of the expansion of mercury to the manufacture of thermometers 681.253 65

530's   *See* **Form Divisions E**

530.8   *History*   Before Edition 13 the Office used 530.8 instead of 530.78 for measuring instruments

            See also **389.1**

531   *See* **General Principles** IX **A** (1) (b) 2, IX **C**

532   *See* **General Principles** IX **C**

532.1   *See* **General Principles** IX **A** (1) (b) 2

533   *See* **General Principles** IX **A** (1) (b) 2

534.8   *History*   Before Edition 16 the Office used 534.8 instead of 620.102 for acoustical engineering

537.6   *See* **General Principles** VIII

537.8   *See* 500's

540.72   *History*   Before Edition 16 the Office used 540.72 instead of 542 for comprehensive chemical laboratory manuals

541.2   *History*   Before Edition 15 the Office used 541.2 instead of subdivisions of 539.7 for nuclear fission or "atomic energy"

542.2–542.7 Include here standards, specifications, operation, use of the various specific chemical laboratory instruments; but class use of a specific instrument in, or application of a specific process to, a specific application, with the application, *e.g.,* distillation of alcoholic beverages **663.5**

543–545 Note the following distinctions in the analysis of a specific substance:

(1) Include in **543.1–543.6** chemical analysis of a specific substance to determine both *what* it contains and *how much*

(2) Include in **544** analysis of a specific substance to determine *what* is in it, but not how much. If a specific method of analysis is used, class in the appropriate subdivision of **544**

(3) Include in **545** analysis of a specific substance to determine *how much* it contains of each of its component parts. If a specific method of analysis is used, class in the appropriate subdivision of **545**

(4) If the substance is known or suspected to contain *carbon* compounds, then its analysis is *organic* analysis; class in **547.3** or its appropriate subdivision

(5) If the analysis is made to determine how much of a *specific component* the substance contains, class with the component in **546–547**

(6) If the analysis is made to determine the *safety* of a specific substance from a public health standpoint, class in the appropriate subdivision of **614**

(7) If the analysis is made to determine, or help to determine, the substance's *effectiveness*, class with its use, *e.g.,* the effectiveness of an insecticide in agriculture **632.951**

(8) If the analysis is made to determine whether the substance has been manufactured according to specifications, class with the manufacture

546–547 *See* **530–559; 543–545** (5)

546 *See* **548**

547   *See* 548

547.3   *See* 543–545 (4)

548   Note that crystal structure of a specific chemical element goes in the appropriate subdivision of 546, of a chemical compound in 546–547, of a natural mineral in 549

549   *See* 530–559; 548

550's   *See* **General Principles** v **B**; **910's**

551   Include in this number and appropriate subdivisions the scientific aspects of geophysical phenomena, *e.g.*, volcanic eruptions, earthquakes, tornadoes; but class their relationship to specific activities with the subject, *e.g.*, of dust storms to soil conservation 631.45. Include in the 900's the general effects of specific geophysical events on people, *e.g.*, San Francisco earthquake and fire 979.461

551.5   *See* **General Principles** ix **D** (2)

551.501 48   Class here weather codes with both meteorological and climatological terms; include in 551.591 codes containing only weather terms

551.55–551.59   Class in 551.59 climate, climatology, weather, using 09+ when limited geographically. Class in 551.55–551.573 8 specific phenomena whether treated as part of meteorology or of climate or of weather

551.591   Include here weather lore, weather signs, weather stations and observations

             See also 551.501 48

553   Class here the natural occurrence and distribution in the earth of mineral substances of economic value, but in 338.2

the economic aspects of the industries which extract the minerals

See also **530–559**

553.097 3   *See* **Form Divisions E**

554–559   *See* **General Principles** x **A**

557.3   *See* **Form Divisions E**

570's   Note that 571–573 relate to man: 571 to his prehistoric activities and artifacts, 572–573 to his prehistoric and historic origin and development. But 574–579 relate to all living organisms treated comprehensively (also, where noted, *e.g.,* 575.1, to man specifically)

571   Note that 571 is used for the scientific study of the material remains of human life and activities of the period prior to recorded history; class in 913 the early historic period and both periods treated together

     See also **570's; 573**

572–573   *See* **570's**

572.4   *See* **573.2–573.3**

573   Class here early man himself, but in 571 his implements and other artifacts

573.2–573.3   Class in 573.2 *how* man originated, in 572.4 *where* he originated, in 573.3 *when* he originated and his development since

573.6   *History*   Before Edition 15 the Office used 573.6 instead of 364.12 for fingerprints and fingerprinting of criminals

574–579   *See* **570's**

574   *History*   Before Edition 15 a note here provided for division of 574 like 581 and 591. Editions 15 and 16 omitted this note but printed under 574 such subdivisions from 581 and 591 as were deemed appropriate

574.8   Class here the study of very small parts, such as cells and tissue structure, of living organisms of any size; in 576 the study of organisms of very small size; in 578 manipulatory techniques in using microscopes for biological study

574.9   *See* 579.6

575.1   *See* 570's

576   *See* 574.8

578   *See* 500's; 574.8

579.6   Class here comprehensive works on methods of collecting and transporting both live and dead specimens. Include in 574.9, 581.9, 591.9 accounts of expeditions for hunting and collecting when the emphasis is on observation and description of the specimens in their habitats; when the expedition is for a specific specimen, class such accounts with the specimen, *e.g.*, elephants 599.61, orchids 584.15. Include in 914–919 accounts of expeditions which emphasize geography and description of the terrain; class in 508.3–508.9 comprehensive works on scientific travels. Class in 778.932 "hunting" of animals with camera, and in 799.2 hunting of animals with gun

581.508 and 591.508   Include here popular works, plant and animal "stories" based not on folklore but on scientific fact. Class such works limited to a specific group or species of plant or animal with the group or species

581.9   *See* 579.6

591.5   Note that 591.51 is limited to behavioral patterns of many kinds. Class both behavioral and nonbehavioral patterns of many kinds in 591.5 without subdivision, both behavioral and nonbehavioral patterns of specific kinds in 591.52–591.59

591.508   *See* 581.508 and 591.508

591.9   *See* 579.6

600 Technology (Applied Science)

600's vs. 700's   Note that the distinction between these Classes is implied in their former headings, "Useful Arts" and "Fine Arts." Just as the 600's "Applied Science" make practical application of the 500's "Pure Science," so the 700's make esthetic application of the 600's. *Examples:* (1) 710 uses the techniques of 620, 630, 690 for the beautification of man's surroundings; (2) 740 uses the techniques of 640, 660–680 for decorative rather than purely utilitarian purposes

600's   *See* **309.22; 338.058; 338.1–338.4; 355–359 A; 380's B; 500's; 630's; 650's B**

605.8   *See* **338.058**

607.2   *See* **658.57**

611–612   *See* **500's**

611   *See* **General Principles** XI **B**

612   *See* **613.8 A**

612.014 46   *History*   Before Edition 16 the Office used **612.014 46** instead of **613.8** for effects of alcohol on health. *See also* **613.8 A**

613.47   *History*   Before Edition 15 the Office used **613.47** instead of **614.7** or **614.796** for public health control of public swimming pools

613.49   *History*   Before Edition 16 the Office used **613.49** instead of **617.601** and **617.701** for oral and optical hygiene respectively

613.5   *See* **General Principles** IX **A** (1) (a) 1

613.71   Include here the relation of exercises to health, in 796.41 description of the exercises

613.8 A   Include here the effects of alcohol and narcotics on man's personal health; but class in 612 purely scientific studies of their effect on the physiology of the body as a whole, and in the appropriate subdivisions of 612 their effects on specific parts of the body. *See also* 612.014 46

      B   Include here how to break the smoking habit

613.94   *History*   Before Edition 16 the Office used 613.94 instead of 364.42 for sterilization of criminals

614   *See* 543–545 (6)

614.073   *History*   Before Edition 15 the Office used 614.073 instead of 610.734 for public health nursing

614.08   *History*   Before Edition 14 provided under 614 regular Form Divisions 074 for exhibitions and 078 for appliances, the Office used 614.08 for both

614.1   *See* 312

614.2   Include here government control and support of medical service, *e.g.*, National Health Service of Great Britain 614.209 42; in 368.42 government-sponsored insurance to provide medical service

614.3   *See* 338.14

615   Include in 615.7 the use of a specific drug to obtain a specific type of effect; in 616 its use in treatment of a specific disease; in 615.2–615.3 its uses in treatment of various diseases and to obtain various effects

615.106 9   Include here pharmacy as a profession in its broad sense; class in 615.406 9 the occupation of compounding and dispensing prescriptions. When in doubt, prefer 615.106 9

615.2–615.3   *See* **615**

615.406 9   *See* **615.106 9**

615.7   *See* **615**

616   Note that surgical treatment of diseases included in subdivisions of **616** goes in the appropriate subdivision of **617**, *e.g.,* surgical treatment of pulmonary tuberculosis **617.542**. *Exception:* surgical treatment of malignant neoplasms **616.994**

   See also **312.26; 312.3; 615**

616.994–616.995   *See* **General Principles** XI B

616.994   *See* **616**

617–618   *See* **312.26; 312.3**

617   *See* **616**

617.542   *See* **616**

619   *History*   Before *Notes and Decisions,* Second Series, No. 7, January 1944, the Office used **619** instead of **636.089** for veterinary science, with the latter as an alternative number

620   *History*   Before Edition 16 the Office used **620** instead of **624** for civil engineering

   See also **385–388 A; 600's vs. 700's** (1); **630's**

620.01–620.09   These correspond to the subdivisions of **000 3** in the table "000 Miscellaneous common subdivisions" in Editions 13 and 14; they do not correspond to the table "00 Viewpoints." Note that they conflict with the normal form divisions **620.26, 620.27, 620.83, 620.84**, under which references appear

620.09   *History*   Before Edition 16 the Office used 620.09 instead of 620.001 49 for techniques of report writing

620.26, 620.27, 620.83, 620.84   *See* 620.01–620.09

621   *History*   Note that Edition 14 provided for division of 621.0 and 621.10 like 620.0. *See* 620.01–620.09

621.01   *See* **Form Divisions F**

621.101   *History*   Before Edition 15 the Office used 621.101 instead of 621.01 for comprehensive works on engineering thermodynamics

621.300 1–621.300 9   Note that these correspond to the two-0 subdivisions under 620. *See* 620.01–620.09

621.300 2   *History*   Before Edition 16 the Office used 621.300 2 instead of 657.838 for accounting in electric utilities

621.313   *See* **General Principles** VIII

621.384   *History*   Note that Editions 13 and 14 included subdivisions of 621.384 000 3 which are similar to 621.300 1–621.300 9

621.384 000 367   *History*   Before Edition 16 the Office used 621.384 000 367 instead of 621.384 18 for radio repairing

621.385   *History*   Before Edition 16 the Office used 621.385 instead of 384.13 and 657.838 for telephone rates and accounting respectively

621.7   *History*   Formerly the Office used 621.7 and its subdivisions for various topics which, according to Edition 16, go in 670–680

621.8   *History*   Before Edition 16 the Office used 621.8 instead of 629.8 for engineering aspects of automation

622.12–622.18 Note that specific minerals in 622.18 take precedence over specific methods and operations in 622.12–622.15

622.2–622.6, 622.8 Note that specific minerals in 622.33–622.39 take precedence over specific methods and operations in 622.2–622.32; but that the subjects dealt with in 622.4–622.6, 622.8 take precedence over specific minerals, *e.g.*, ventilation in coal mines 622.42, but open-pit mining of coal 622.33

622.34 *See* **General Principles** IX A (1) (a) 2

622.8 *See* 622.2–622.6, 622.8

623 A Class here engineering aspects of military science, including how to construct and operate military matériel, its mechanism and efficiency; but class in 355–359 the organization of the forces that use the matériel, and its application to warfare. Use 355–359 as the comprehensive numbers

B When both military and civil aspects of specific engineering operations are treated together without discernible emphasis, class with the civil aspect; when military aspects are emphasized, class in 623 and its subdivisions. *Examples:* manufacture of military aircraft 623.74, of civil aircraft 629.133, of both 629.133; military sanitary engineering 623.75, civil sanitary engineering 628, both 628. *Exceptions:* comprehensive works on small firearms for both military and nonmilitary uses 623.44; military naval engineering, nonmilitary naval engineering, and comprehensive works 623.8

C Class in 623 the topics of military engineering as applied to many wars or to no specific war, but class in the 900's a topic limited to one war, *e.g.*, siege operations at Vicksburg 973.734 4

623.19 Include here technical planning, construction, use of specific forts; but class comprehensive histories of specific forts with local history

623.44   *See* 623 **B**

623.6   *See* 355.27

623.74, 623.75, 623.8   *See* 623 **B**

624   *History*   Note that the 14th and earlier editions provided
              for division of 624.0 and 624.00 like 620. and 620.0. *See*
              620.01–620.09

624.550 974 72   *See* **General Principles** xx **A**

625   *History*   Note that the 14th and earlier editions provided
              for division of 625.0 and 625.00 like 620. and 620.0. *See*
              620.01–620.09

625.18   *See* 385.2–385.3

625.2   *See* 385.2–385.3

625.263   *See* **General Principles** viii

627.1   *History*   Before Edition 15 the Office used 627.1 instead
              of 627 for comprehensive works on river and valley engi-
              neering

628   *See* 623 **B**

628.1   *History*   Before Edition 15 the Office used 628.1 instead
              of 333.91 for comprehensive works on water resources

629.133   *See* 623 **B**

629.134 53   *See* 920's **B**

629.138   *History*   Before Edition 16 directed that specific applica-
              tions of aircraft go with the subject the Office used subdivi-
              sions of 629.138

629.281   *History*   Before Edition 16 the Office used 629.281 instead of 914–919 for touring guides which included little description

630's   Note that the techniques of the 630's apply scientific knowledge from many parts of the 500's, and techniques from other parts of the 600's, such as 620, 690, to the raising of plants and animals for profit or pleasure. The resulting products may be used directly in the home (640's) or undergo commercial processing (660–680) into articles required in carrying on various useful arts (600's) and fine arts (700's). Note also that the 630's include some parts of the processing now or formerly performed on or near the farm, such as making butter (637.2) and cheese (637.3)

See also **338.1; 600's vs. 700's** (1)

630.58   *See* **338.058**

631–632   Note that, when any topic included in 631–632 is limited to a specific product or group of products, it goes with the product in 633–639

631.5   *See* **General Principles** ix **A** (2) 2

631.56   *See* **338.14**

633–639   *See* **338.14; 631–632**

633.15   *See* **General Principles** v **A** (1)

633.510 58   *See* **338.058**

634.98   *History*   Before Edition 16 the Office used 634.98 instead of 674.12 for identification of woods

635.9   *See* **712–718**

636.77   *See* **700's C**

637.2–637.3   *See* 630's

640's   *See* 600's vs. 700's (2); 630's

641.5–641.87   Include here, where applicable, preparation of raw or unheated foods for the table

641.5   Note that, since most cookbooks consist chiefly of recipes, Form Division 083 is not used for them

641.631   *History*   Before Edition 15 the Office used 641.631 instead of 664.75 for commercial baking

645   Include here the choice, placing, and use of furnishings from the standpoint of suitability, utility, convenience, economy. Include in 747 the decoration of interiors, and in 749 furniture and accessories, from the standpoint of beauty and harmony. When in doubt, prefer 747 and 749

646.069   *History*   Before Edition 15 provided 687 and Edition 16 provided 659.152 for fashion modeling the Office used 646.069

646.2   *See* 680's B

649.1   *See* 136.7

649.6   *See* 395.1

650's   *In order to understand fully all the statements that follow on 650–659, refer not only to Edition 16 but also to* Decimal Classification Additions, Notes, and Decisions, *v. 1, no. 10/11*

650's   A   "Business" may be considered as comprising those enterprises which (1) buy and sell goods, and/or (2) sell services, *e.g.*, dry cleaning firms, and/or (3) manufacture or produce goods at any level from primary extraction, *e.g.*, agriculture, to completion of consumer products. "Industry" is, generally speaking, the same as definition (3), altho (2) is sometimes considered "light industry"

B   For DC purposes, "business enterprises" are those enterprises of the kind described above whose techniques go in the 600's. This excludes, among others, newspaper publishing 070.3, banking and allied enterprises 332.1–332.3, real estate business 333.33, insurance business 368, public utilities and public services 380, jewelry business 739.27, concert management business 780.65, music stores 780.658 (but not manufacture of musical instruments 681.81), motion picture entertainment industry 791.43. It also excludes various enterprises which are not commercial in nature, but which do, nevertheless, use business methods, engage in business activities, and have business offices, *e.g.*, libraries, museums, churches, prisons, schools. All these exclusions may be called, for classification purposes, "nonbusiness enterprises"

C   "Business methods" are specific methods which have been evolved to promote the ends of business enterprises (even if used also by nonbusiness enterprises), *e.g.*, personnel management

650.62   *History*   Before Edition 16 the Office used 650.62 instead of 366 for Rotary, Kiwanis, Lions, and similar businessmen's service clubs

651.02   Class here "secretaries' handbooks" dealing broadly with office management from the point of view of the "boss's secretary," but include in 651.7 those limited to or primarily concerned with correspondence. Class in 651.374 1 job descriptions of secretarial positions intended for the use of management

651.374 1   *See* **651.02**

651.7   Include here the technique of writing to accomplish business and managerial purposes, in 808.066 the technique of presenting technical matter in writing, in 029.6 the preparation of written matter for publication

See also **651.02**

651.74   Include in subdivisions of this number works giving spelling and vocabulary specifically for the secretary

651.9   Note that subdivisions of this number are used only for works dealing with all or several subdivisions of **651** in relation to specific business and nonbusiness enterprises. In accordance with the general principle of classification by most specific subject, class a specific aspect of the management of a specific kind of office with the aspect, *e.g.*, management of business records in an insurance office **651.5**. *See* **General Principles** iv

652   *See* **411**

655.1–655.5 Note the unusual structure and arrangement for both printing and publishing: under each, historical works precede descriptive and expository

655.1   Include here establishments the primary or only function of which is printing, and "private presses" whose distribution function is at most secondary. Include in **655.4** those establishments, including university "presses," which are primarily publishers or booksellers. When in doubt, prefer **655.4**

655.32   *See* **General Principles** xv

655.4   *See* **655.1**

655.53   Include here the design or format of the physical book—binding, paper, size, illustrations; but class in **741.64** the art of book illustration, and in **655.7** the techniques of binding

655.58   *See* **028**

655.7   *See* **655.53**

656   *History*   Before Edition 15 relocated transportation from **656** to **385–388**, the Office used **656** as the basis of subdivision for transportation workers, *e.g.*, under **331.28**

658   *See* **338.1–338.4; 658.9**

658.1 **A**   Organization "for control" deals with the ways in which a firm is organized so that its managers may control it. This includes "corporation law" for its establishment and organization

       B   Include here the practical application to the establishment and management of industrial companies of the economic theories and principles considered in **338.7–338.8**

658.3   Note that, altho nontechnical works on personnel management in specific business and nonbusiness enterprises go in 658.3 and its subdivisions, an exception is made of personnel management in public administration, both civil and military, works on which go in the appropriate subdivisions of **351–352, 355–359**

              See also **331 A**

658.312   *See* **658.511**

658.322 2   *See* **658.511**

658.37   Note that subdivisions of this number are used only for works dealing with all or several subdivisions of **658.3** in relation to specific business and nonbusiness enterprises. In accordance with the general principle of classification by most specific subject, class a specific aspect of personnel management of a specific business or nonbusiness enterprise with the aspect, *e.g.,* morale of library employees **658.314**. *See* **General Principles** IV

658.381   Include here rest periods as a part of personnel management, but in **658.544** rest periods in relation to fatigue and monotony

658.511   Class here analysis of a "job" (a piece of work) for promotion of efficiency, in **658.322 2** evaluation of a "job" (the duties of a worker) for determination of its compensation, in 658.312 description of a "job" (the duties of a worker) for use in general personnel management

658.544   *See* 658.381

658.57   Include here research in production management. Class in 607.2 industrial research in general, and research for the development of new products. Research on the value, use, technology of a specific product goes with the product

658.8   *See* 347.42; 658.89

658.88   Include here credit guides which list individuals or firms and indicate their credit standing

658.89   Note that subdivisions of this number are used only for works dealing with all or several subdivisions of **658.8** in relation to specific enterprises. In accordance with the general principle of classification by most specific subject, class a specific aspect of marketing the products of a specific enterprise with the aspect, *e.g.*, sales quotas for automobiles **658.812**. *See* **General Principles** IV

658.896 3 *See* 338.14

658.9   Note that subdivisions of this number are used only for works dealing with all or several subdivisions of **658** in relation to specific enterprises. In accordance with the general principle of classification by most specific subject, class a specific aspect of the management of a specific enterprise with the aspect, *e.g.*, personnel management in mining industry **658.376 22**. *See* **General Principles** IV

659.112   Include here the organization and administration of both (1) advertising firms and (2) advertising departments of firms whose main business is something else

660's–680's   *History*   It will help the classifier to understand the distinctions among these three Divisions if he remembers that the three-figure subdivisions were made in the 19th century. At that time, those products included in the 660's involved chemical reactions or similar processes, those in the 670's involved the use of machinery, and those in the 680's (then called "mechanic trades") involved work done by hand. In the latter half of the 20th century these distinctions no longer hold; chemical and machine processing in manufacture has spread, and work by hand has almost disappeared

See also 600's vs. 700's (2); 630's

669   *See* **General Principles** IX A (1) (a) 2

669.1   *See* **General Principles** IX B

670's   *See* **General Principles** IX A (2) 3; 660's–680's

671–673   *See* **General Principles** IX A (1) (a) 2

672   *See* **General Principles** IX B

676   *See* **General Principles** IX A (2) 3

677.210 58   *See* 338.058

680's   A   Include hand or home construction of various articles with their manufacture, unless specifically provided for elsewhere, *e.g.*, hand construction of violins 787.12, handwoven fabrics 746.1

B   Generally the distinction between home technology and home handicraft is based on creativity. Include in the 680's amateur manuals on work following more or less predetermined procedures; class in 745.5 manuals which emphasize creative design even if simple. When in doubt, prefer 745.5.

Note also the similar distinction between plain sewing 646.2 and art needlework 746.44

See also 660's–680's

681.134   *History*   Before Edition 15 provided 621.345 and Edition 16 provided 681.844 for manufacture of sound motion-picture apparatus, the Office used 681.134

681.81   *See* 650's B

690's   *See* 600's vs. 700's (1); 630's; 720's

690   *History*   Before Edition 15 provided 680 and Edition 16 provided 688.1 for comprehensive works on modelmaking, the Office used 690

700 The Arts

700's A   Note that, in various parts of this Class, the schedules make provisions, mostly new in Edition 15, which emphasize the major interest of students and historians of art in individual artists, to the possible prejudice of the greater interest of practicing artists and technicians in methods and materials. Thus, all specific painters go in 759.1–759.999 regardless of medium, technique, subject, or period; all sculptors (except ancient), in 730.94–730.999; collections of prints by any specific print maker, in 769.9; collections of drawings by any specific artist, in 741.93–741.999. Note, however, that other kinds of specific artists, *e.g.*, architects, musicians, are not so treated

B   Whenever an artist's work goes in a number with geographic subdivision, carry out to country only, *e.g.*, a sculptor generally associated with California 730.973 *not* 730.979 4

C   Class artistic and pictorial representations and illustrations of a specific subject in the 700's if interest is chiefly artistic, *e.g.*, dogs in art 704.943 2; but class with subject, using Form Division 084 when appropriate, if interest is chiefly in the subject, *e.g.*, illustrations of dogs 636.77. In judging which interest predominates consider (1) whether the author indicates it by a statement of his purpose, (2) whether the text discusses the artistic aspects or the subject, (3) whether the artist is well-known. If emphasis is doubtful, class with the subject. *See* **General Principles** III

    See also **General Principles** XIX; **246–247**; **600's vs. 700's**; **630's**

704.942–704.948 9   Include here rather than in 704.949 specific parts or varieties of each specific subject, *e.g.*, women's hands 704.942 4, vegetables 704.943 4

704.943 2   *See* **700's C**

704.948 5–704.948 7   Include here rather than in 704.948 4 representations of events the central characters of which are those provided for in these numbers, *e.g.,* flight into Egypt 704.948 56

708.1–708.9   Note that the schedule carries geographic division to country only, except to states of the United States 708.14–708.19. This is true also for those numbers, such as 748.29, which are divided like 708.1–708.999

710's   *See* **600's vs. 700's** (1)

711.2–711.4   *See* **309.22–309.26 A**

711.58–711.59   *See* **331.833**

711.58   *See* **General Principles** ix **A** (1) (a) **1**

711.7   Class here planning for the broad objectives of beauty, comfort, convenience, health; include in 385–388 planning for the specific purposes of efficient movement and control of traffic. When in doubt, prefer 385–388

712–718   Class here the planning and design of gardens for beauty and efficiency, in 635.9 the production and care of garden plants

718   Note that this number is limited to administration, planning, design. Class in 718.09+ the design of specific cemeteries, in 914–919 their general description, in 940–999 their history, in 929.5 collections of inscriptions on their tombstones. For national memorial cemeteries (718.8) observe the same distinctions, but class history of a cemetery associated with a specific war with the war

720's   Note that the 690's are used for materials and construction only, the 720's for design, or comprehensive works on design and construction

See also **500's**

720.81   *History*   Before Edition 15 the Office used 720.81 instead of 720.9+ for comprehensive works by and about individual architects

722–724   *History*   Before Edition 15 the Office used 722–724 with direct geographic subdivision instead of 720.9+ for styles of architecture in a specific country

725–728   *See* 914–919 D

730–735   Note that the cross references and notes in the schedules provide, in effect, the following list of preferences to be followed in case of conflict: 730.9+; 732–735; 731.5–731.8; 731.1–731.4. *Examples:* casting sculpture 731.45, casting busts 731.74, busts in a specific gallery but from many periods and places 731.74, 18th century busts 735.21, 18th century French busts 730.944, casting technique used on Houdon's busts 730.944

730.94–730.999   *See* 700's A

730.944   *See* 730–735

730.973   *See* **General Principles xx D; 700's B**

731–735   *History*   Before Edition 15 the Office used 731–735 instead of 730.9+ for individual sculptors

731.45   *See* 730–735

731.74   *See* 730–735

735.21   *See* 730–735

739.27   *See* 650's B

740's   *See* 600's vs. 700's (2)

741.23   Note that drawing with chalk or crayon made of the dried paste called "pastel" is not to be confused with painting in subdued or "pastel" colors. Class the former in 741.23, the latter in the appropriate part of the 750's

741.59   Note that most books of cartoons have some text with each cartoon, in some cases so much that the cartoon is only illustrative of the text. Class in 741.59 collections the text of which is minor, *e.g.*, limited to captions or legends; class with the subject those in which the cartoons are illustrative of the text

741.64   *See* 655.53

741.93–741.999   *See* 700's A

743.4–743.7   Include here rather than in 743.8+ specific parts or varieties of each specific subject, *e.g.*, hands 743.4, vegetables 743.7

745.5   *See* 680's B

746.1   *See* 680's A

746.44   *See* 680's B

747   *See* 645

748.29   *See* 708.1–708.9

749   *See* 645

750's   Note that the cross references and notes in the schedules provide, in effect, the following list of preferences to be followed in case of conflict: 759.1–759.999; 759.01–759.06; 751–751.6 and 752; 753–758.7; 751.7; 758.9. *Examples:* collections of many kinds of paintings 758.9, collections of murals of many times and places 751.73, landscape murals 758.1, technique of painting murals (or landscape murals) 751.4, technique of painting murals in fresco 751.44, frescoes of the Renaissance 759.03, Renaissance frescoes of Italy 759.5, frescoes of Michelangelo 759.5

See also 500's; 741.23

750.1   *See* **Form Division 01**

751–758   *History*   Before Edition 15 the Office used 751–758 instead of 759.1–759.999 for individual painters

751.4   *See* 750's

751.73   *See* 750's

753–758.7   Include in 753–757.9 and in 758.1–758.7, rather than in 758 undivided, specific parts or varieties of each specific subject, *e.g.*, women's hands 757.4, vegetables 758.42

     History   Before Edition 16 the Office used 753–758.7 instead of 751 for materials and methods of painting specific subjects

757.4   *See* 753–758.7

758.1   *See* 750's

758.42   *See* 753–758.7

758.9   *See* 750's

759   *See* **General Principles** xix

759.03   *See* 750's

759.1–759.999   *See* 700's A

759.4   *See* **Form Division 01**

759.5   *See* 750's

761–767   *History*   Before Edition 16 the Office used 761–767 instead of 769.9 for works of individual engravers

769.9   *See* **700's A**

770's   *See* **500's; 910's**

770.2   *History*   Before Edition 16 the Office used 770.2 instead of 771.31 for guides to the operation of specific cameras

778.315   *See* **General Principles xv**

778.932   *See* **579.6**

780's   Note that the physical nature of musical scores and parts, as well as their use, makes it advisable in most libraries to separate them on the shelves from works about music. Until Edition 16, no special provision was made for them except the suggestion that the same numbers might be used for works about music and the music itself, prefixing **M** or **MS** to numbers when used for the latter. In order to provide separately for scores and parts, Edition 16 makes certain modifications under 780.8 for collected scores, and adds expansions under the various kinds and mediums of music in 782–789. Only under 780.8 is it necessary to adjust the use of numbers from that provided in previous editions: in order to limit 780.81–780.84 to collected scores, other topics included there in Edition 14 drop back to 780.8. Also, before Edition 16 the Office used 780.81 instead of 780.92 for criticism and appraisal of individual musicians. Note (1) that, as indicated by cross references under 780.15 and 780.92, criticism of works of individual musicians, when limited to a specific kind of music, goes in the number for the kind with Form Division 081, *e.g.*, criticism of Bach's sacred cantatas 783.408 1; (2) that criticism of a specific composition goes, not with the composition itself, *i.e.*, the score, but with works about the kind of music, *e.g.*, a work about Beethoven's *Fifth Symphony* goes in 785.110 81 *not* 785.115 4

780.15	*See* 780's
780.65	*See* 650's **B**
780.8	*See* 780's
780.9	*See* 781.7
780.92	*See* 780's
780.956 93	*See* 781.7
781.1	*See* 500's

781.15   Class here the emotional and intellectual effect of sounds put together in pleasing or orderly fashion, but in 152.2 the threshold and intelligibility of sound and its perception in terms of pitch and quality

781.7   Class here works on the music that is typical of, or indigenous to, a specific race or country; class in 780.9 works on music in a country, including the music composed or performed there, regardless of country of origin. *Examples:* "Jews in music," their contribution as composers, performers, conductors 780.956 93; secular and religious music typical of Jews thru the ages 781.756 93; Chinese music 781.751

781.96   Class here works on the words written to be sung or said with dramatic music, or for which such music is written, including the techniques of writing. Include here also collections of such poetry and prose when they are not limited to a specific kind of dramatic music

782–789   *See* 780's

783   *History*   Before Edition 14 the Office used 783:281–783:289 for music of specific denominations and 783:292–783:299 for music of other specific religions, instead of 783.026 and 783.029 respectively

          See also 264.1–264.9

783.9   *See* 245 A

784   Note that "hillbilly" songs are usually mixtures of several of
             the kinds of songs in 784.1–784.7, and that, therefore, works
             about them should go in 784 and appropriate subdivisions
             thereof, and collections of them in 784.8

784.6–784.7 Class in 784.61–784.660 6 songs composed, compiled or ap-
             propriate for special groups of singers, *e.g., Trinity College
             Song Book* 784.622 06; class in 784.68 songs limited to a spe-
             cific subject, *e.g.,* labor songs 784.683 31; class in 784.7
             songs in which the source or origin is of special significance

784.61   Note that some collections are so inclusive that it is difficult
             to choose between this number and 784.8. When in doubt,
             prefer 784.8

784.68   Note that here, because of the "divide-like" feature, scores
             and parts are not given separate numbers

784.7   Note that, in this number and its subdivisions, only 784.756
             makes separate provision for scores and parts

             See also 784.6–784.7

784.8   *See* 784; 784.61

784.93   *See* 421.5

787.12   *See* 680's A

791.3   Class here only those trained animal performances con-
             nected with the circus, and in 791.8 other trained animal
             performances

791.4 and 792   Include in these numbers and their subdivisions scripts
             for production purposes; in the 800's stage, motion-picture,
             radio, television plays to be read as literature. Class here
             also production scripts adapted from literary works, *e.g.,* a
             script of *Hamlet* for television 791.457

791.43   *See* 650's **B**

791.6   *See* 394

791.8   *See* 791.3

792   *History*   Before Edition 15 the Office used 792 instead of the 800's for motion-picture, radio, and television plays

                See also **791.4 and 792**

793.74–793.8   Include here collections of trick problems, paradoxes, puzzles, and the like, based on scientific facts but used for entertainment with no serious attempt to explain the tricks on a scientific basis. Class with the specific science, using Form Division 076 where applicable, collections of scientific problems used for teaching and study, *e.g.*, mathematical problems 510.76

793.8   *History*   Before Edition 15 the Office used 793.8 instead of 795.438 for amateur card tricks

796   *See* 371.74–371.75

796.41   *See* 613.71

796.7   *See* 910's

797.1   *See* 910's

799.2   *See* 579.6; 910's

800 Literature (Belles-Lettres)

800's A   In determining the period number for an individual author, use the period of the author's earliest known belletristic publication. As a rule of thumb to determine this, use the copyright date of the earliest work in the library. When in doubt, follow the copyright date of the work in hand

B   Note that some legendary or historical themes, such as the search for the Holy Grail or the battle of Roland with the Saracens, appear as the basis for medieval literary works, often anonymous; then, later, as the basis for works in many literatures, periods, and forms. In such cases it is the theme rather than the literature that continues. Class each retelling with the literature, form, and period in which it is written; class in **809.93** works about the theme as treated in literature; class with the subject (frequently in a subdivision of **398**) works about the theme apart from its literary treatment

C   Note that fiction, whatever its subject or type, goes in subdivision 3 under the appropriate literature; *e.g.*, early 20th century French detective stories **843.912**, but history and criticism **843.912 093** (in accord with directions under **809.9**). Note, however, that the Office does not classify current fiction in English

See also **General Principles** IV, XII, XIX; **040's B; 291.82; 427; 791.4 and 792**

800's Form Divisions   Note that collections from and about specific literatures and literary forms should be examined carefully to determine their true content and purpose. For example, class in Form Division **09** collections of history and criticism; in Form Division **082** collections by several authors *from* a literature or literary form, also collections both *from* and *about*. But class collections of works of one author in one literary form in the appropriate number without form division, *e.g.*, collected plays of Eugene O'Neill **812.52**; and

118

collections of works of one author in several literary forms in the appropriate "miscellany" number, *e.g.*, collected works (fiction, drama, poetry) of Victor Hugo 848.8

801.9   *See* **Form Division 01**

806   Class here societies devoted to literature ("literary societies"); in 808.006 societies devoted to writing, *e.g.*, authors' clubs

807   Class here teaching of general literature, and in 808.07 teaching of literary composition. Class teaching of a specific literature with that literature

808   *See* **420.7**

808.006   *See* **806**

808.066   *See* **651.7**

808.07   *See* **807**

808.1   *See* **426**

808.5   *See* **401.8**

808.52   *See* **421.5**

808.831   Class here collections of short stories from many literatures; but note that there are no specific numbers for short stories from specific literatures, and that, therefore, such collections must go with other fiction from those literatures

809.9   *See* **800's C**

809.93   *See* **800's B**

810's   Note that, since English is the parent literature, works treating more or less equally of American and English literature go in the 820's

811.52 *See* **Form Division 01**

814.52 *See* **040's B**

816 Include here, and in subdivision **6** under other literatures, only those letters which are compiled to be read for their literary value and enjoyment, and are not on a specific subject. Class as biography those collections of letters which are compiled to show the life and personality of the writer; class letters on a specific subject with the subject, *e.g.*, letters by an early 20th century American poet on his own poetry 811.52, on foreign relations of the United States and Great Britain 327.730 42

820's *See* **810's**

833 *See* **General Principles** XII

851.1 *See* **General Principles** XII

900 History

900's A   Note that position on the map, rather than political affiliation or inclusion, usually determines the number assigned to the history of a specific place or area. While political affiliation may change, position on the map is stable. Stability is especially important in local history, and as the basis for building numbers for description and for geographic subdivision thruout the schedules. For example, Editions 1–14 all enumerated 991–996 as Malaysia, Sunda, Australasia, Australia, New Guinea, Polynesia and Micronesia, respectively. Each of these is a recognizable geographic group of islands, altho their political affiliations have been and continue to be most diverse, *e.g.*, Philippines (a part of Malaysia) under Spain, then under the United States, then independent. Editions 15 and 16, while retaining the geographic groupings, use current terminology

B   In determining numbers to be used for comprehensive works on geographical features, such as mountains, rivers, valleys, which cut across several countries, states, or other entities that have separate numbers, apply the following principles: (1) Class in the most specific number that will contain the feature, *e.g.*, class in 974 the Connecticut River, which touches four of the Northeastern states. (2) But if choice of such a number would place the feature in the same number with works much broader in scope than the feature itself, class it with the area (a) which contains most of it, or (b) which contains the most important part of it, or (c) which comes first in the schedules. *Examples:* Amazon River, which is mostly in northern Brazil, 981.1 *not* 980; Nile River, the most important part of which economically is in Egypt, 962 *not* 960; Cayuga Lake, New York, which forms part of the boundary line between Cayuga and Seneca Counties, 974.768 *not* 974.76

See also **355–359 B; 400's C; 551**

900's Period Divisions   Class works treating of several consecutive history period divisions according to the general principles for classing works dealing with more than one subject. *See* **General Principles VI.** Note that the emphasis on the several periods sometimes is not equal, *e.g.,* the first and last of the periods may be treated only partially or incidentally. *Examples:* Class medieval world history 476–1453 in **909,** modern world history 1453–date in **909,** world history of early Middle Ages 476–1000 in **909.1,** of late Middle Ages 1200–1453 in **909.2** unless emphasis is elsewhere, world history 1648–1715 in **909.6** unless emphasis is elsewhere

900's Wars

A   Class a war with the history of the country where most of the fighting took place. If, when a war starts, it is impossible to know where most of the fighting will take place or how many countries will be involved, use the best judgment of the moment in assigning a number. *Example:* World Wars I and II were, on this basis, first considered European wars and placed in **940** instead of **909**

B   Be careful lest, while a war is in progress and authors, librarians, and public are preoccupied with it, works are placed with the war because they deal with the war period *even tho not about the war, e.g.,* higher education in United States as affected by World War II **378.73** *not* **940.53** or any of its subdivisions

C   Note that works on a specific battle or action in a war go with the war, not with the history of the place where the action occurred, *e.g.,* 1945 air raids on Tokyo **940.544 2** *not* **952.135**

D   Note that personal narratives relating to a war and limited to a specific subject, *e.g.,* a specific campaign, go with the subject. Class in the "personal narratives" numbers, *e.g.,*

940.548, only those narratives, individual or collected, which cannot be so limited

See also **355–359 B; 355.09; 623 C; 920's B**

909, 930–999   History, as included here, is a record, usually chronological, of events which have happened to mankind and in which man has taken part; works on history may be limited as to time or period covered, as to place, or both. History limited as to subject goes with the specific subject, with Form Division **09** where applicable, *e.g.*, economic history of United States 330.973; but note that some works whose titles imply subject limitation are in content so inclusive that they are not actually so limited. *Examples:* (1) "Political history" generally includes accounts of political events such as successive political administrations, changes in political affiliation, their causes and effects, and goes in 909, 930–999 (tho "political history" limited to such purely political matters as party politics and elections goes in the 320's). (2) "Military history" usually includes accounts of wars, their economic and political causes and effects, diplomatic relations involved, and goes in the 900's (tho "military history" limited to military analysis of campaigns, battles, wars goes in 355.48)

909   *See* **900's Period Divisions**

909.82   *See* **940's**

910's   Include here accounts of voyages, tours, hunting or photographic trips, and the like, which are primarily records of the events of the trip and general descriptions of the country thru which it is made. Class in 797.1, 796.7, 799.2, the 770's, the 550's, works which emphasize the techniques of boating, automobiling, hunting, photography, geological prospecting

913   Include here archeology of historic times; but class in the early period subdivisions of 930–999, *e.g.*, in 932.01, works

which combine archeological and other records into consecutive historical narratives

See also **417; 571**

914–919 **A** Include here (1) description, (2) geography, (3) travel, when limited by place: (1) By *description* is meant the portrayal of man's situation, way of life, culture, civilization, total customs, at a given time in a given place. (2) *Geography* describes the earth: land, air, water, and whatever lives on or in them. (3) A work of *travel* tells where the traveler goes, what he does, and what he sees. Class these three, when limited by subject, with the specific subject, using Form Division 09 where applicable to indicate local treatment. *Examples:* Marriage customs in Japan 392.509 52; economic geography of United States 330.973; travel in Arizona to gather geological information 557.91. *See also* **910's**

B Include here travel or accounts of life in specific places in earlier as well as in modern times. Note that it is possible to add period divisions from 940–999 to these numbers, even tho the Office has not done so

C Include here comprehensive works dealing with both history (940–999) and description (914–919) of a place, unless the emphasis is on history. Use 914–919 as the most comprehensive numbers for works on specific places

D Include here descriptions of or guides to historic buildings. Class in 940–999 the history of historic buildings as related to the history of the places in which located. Class in 725–728 architecture of the buildings. Class an historic building which has become an organized historical museum with the history of the place for which the building serves as a museum, using Form Division 074 where applicable, *e.g.,* a museum of Minnesota history 977.600 74

See also **Form Divisions F; 301.2; 309.1; 352.03–352.09; 579.6; 718; 940–999**

919.9   *See* 940–999

920's A   Note that the Office does not add form divisions to 920–928, altho it uses geographic subdivision when specified in the schedules

B   Class biographies, diaries, personal narratives, and the like, written for the express purpose of narrating the history of a series of events or to illustrate a subject, with the event or the subject, *e.g.,* personal narrative of World War II prison escape 940.547 2+, diary of a test pilot 629.134 53

C   Class as biographies works giving approximately equal emphasis to the lives of specific persons and to the history and criticism of their work

See also **General Principles** XIII (1), XIX; **816**

920.01–920.02   Note that, to be "universal," a collective biography must be very inclusive. When in doubt, prefer 920.02

920.1–928
A   Note that this is generally but not completely divided like the whole classification, and that many but not all of the subdivisions are further divided geographically. Do not divide geographically without specific provision, because this blocks future subject division. Since many people important enough to be the subject of biographies live and work in more than one place, it is not advisable to carry geographic division beyond country. Similarly, since, in many subject fields, most people do not specialize too intensely, it is not advisable to divide the subjects too narrowly; *e.g.,* a musician may be a violinist, composer, and conductor in turn, but always a musician 927.8

B   Class the biography of a person (or persons) according to the profession, business, service, or other activity in which, for good or bad, he made his greatest contribution to the world, or which occupied the greatest or most significant part of his life. Add geographic subdivision (when the schedules so provide) for the country in which he lived the longest or carried on his greatest or most significant activity. For *exception, see* **923.1 B.** *Examples:* (1) Lives of most statesmen go in 923.2, a statesman's main contribution usually being in that capacity, even tho his earlier life may have been devoted to some other field. Sometimes, however, a person whose life's work is in a different field may be a member of a legislature for only a short time; in such cases the main field may be used to determine his biography number. (2) A financier or capitalist turned philanthropist or humanitarian is likely to be more noted for the latter, in which case his biography goes in 923.6. When in doubt, prefer 923.6 to 923.3. (3) A teacher's main contribution usually is as an educator, but if his contribution to the subject field in which he taught is outstanding his biography goes with the subject. When in doubt, prefer **923.7**

922   Class the biography of a missionary in the subdivision for the denomination which he represents, adding geographic subdivision for the country in which he has longest been a missionary or performed his most significant work. Biographies of those missionaries serving under interdenominational boards of missions go in 922 without further subdivision

See also **General Principles** XIX

923   Note that this is subdivided broadly like the 300's, except for 923.1 and 923.9. Consultation of the 300 schedule sometimes helps in determining what goes in the various subdivisions

923.1 A   Include here biographies of both reigning monarchs and their consorts

B   Note that this number takes precedence over all other numbers for individual biographies, *e.g.*, a biography of a president of the United States goes in 923.173 even tho the greater part of his life is spent in education, law, military service, or some other field

See also 923

923.173   *See* 923.1 **B**; 929.2 (2)

923.2   *See* 920.1–928 **B** (1); 929.2 (1)

923.6   *See* 920.1–928 **B** (2)

923.7   *See* 920.1–928 **B** (3)

923.9   *See* 923

927–927.7   *History*   Until Edition 16 the Office included here, with an alternative number from the 700's, those works about individual artists which are part biography and part criticism

929.2   Include here family histories in narrative form, as well as those consisting of genealogical tables. But note (1) that a family history which is, in effect, collective biography of persons prominent in the same subject field goes with the subject, *e.g.*, a family of statesmen 923.2; and (2) that a "family history" in which the history is background for and subordinate to the life of its most prominent member goes with biography of that member, *e.g.*, the forebears, family, and life (with life emphasized) of a president of the United States 923.173

929.5   *See* 718

930–999   **A**   Include with history of a country or locality works which combine history and biography, or history and genealogy, or all three. Include also source materials and archival records, unless they relate to a specific subject

      B   Class histories limited by both place and period in the number for the specific place followed by the subdivision for the specific period, if the schedules provide for period division. *Exception:* Some works on the early history of a country, such as a colonial period, may be limited geographically in coverage, and yet be so essential a part of the history of the whole country that they logically belong in the colonial period of the country's history, *e.g.,* settlement of Plymouth Colony 973.22 *not* 974.48. When in doubt, prefer local history

See also 909, 930–999; 913

930–999 Form Divisions   Note that under all geographical areas, large and small, except Ireland 941.5 and United States 973, period subdivisions are discriminated from place subdivisions by use of 0. Since notation must be left open for future periods, and since period subdivisions may be provided later for areas for which no such provision is currently made in the schedules, the single-0 subdivisions should all be reserved for this purpose, and two 0's should always be used for form divisions. (Note, however, that 970.1–970.6 and 980.1–980.6 have special meanings, and that period divisions, if later set up, will require two 0's, so that form divisions should take three 0's)

933   Note that the distinction between 933 and 939.45 is largely one of historical period, with 939.45 being used for Palestine before the Israelites under Joshua and his successors conquered it, and 933 for Palestine after that time. The dividing line may be considered approximately 1300 B.C.

940–999   Include here works on the early exploration and discovery of a country leading to its settlement or exploitation by civilized peoples, *e.g.,* early exploration of Arizona 979.101; but class in 914–919 accounts of the growth of geographic knowledge stemming from exploring expeditions that have taken place after the basic geography is known and settlement and exploitation have begun, *e.g.,* Powell's trips of discovery along the Colorado River 917.913. (Inasmuch as the Antarctic Regions are not settled, discovery and exploration may reasonably go in 919.9)

See also **335.43; 718; 914–919 C, D**

940's   Note that this Division is limited to history of Europe, and to comprehensive works on history of Europe and those continents settled by Europeans, *i.e.*, the Occident. *Exceptions:* the two World Wars, which no doubt would have been given numbers under 909.82 had their extent been foreseen when the editors set up numbers for them. *See also* **900's Wars A**

940.49   *History*   *See* **973.39**

940.547 2   *See* **920's B**

940.549   *History*   *See* **973.39**

941.5   *See* **930–999 Form Divisions**

970.1–970.6   *See* **930–999 Form Divisions**

972   *See* **General Principles v B**

973   *See* **329.01; 930–999 Form Divisions**

973.1   *History*   Beginning with Edition 6, 1899, an expansion here included explorers whose discoveries were not in territory now included in the United States, or were in territory now included in the United States and also other parts of the Americas; and a specific number, 973.15, was set up for the explorations of Columbus altho they did not touch territory now in the United States. No doubt provision was made here for these early explorations because they were considered an essential part of the beginnings of United States history. Edition 16 directs that discoveries and explorations in a specific country go with that country, and that 973.1 and its subdivisions be limited to comprehensive works on discoveries in the United States, in North America, or in the Americas. Until Edition 16 the Office tended to class in 973.1 and its subdivisions all the explorations listed under those numbers

973.331 2   *See* **General Principles** xx **B**

973.39   *History*   Before Edition 15 the Office used subdivisions of this number instead of the 700's and 800's for music, art, and literary works relating to the Revolutionary War. The same use was made of similar numbers under other wars

973.529, 973.629, 973.79, 973.899   *History*   *See* **973.39**

974–979   Include here boundary disputes between states of the United States, using the number for that state of those involved which comes first in the schedules, and adding the proper period subdivision. Class disputes between counties and/or cities similarly. Class those between countries in **327**

974.201–974.204   *See* **General Principles** x **A**

975.3   *See* **General Principles** xx **C**

980.1–980.6   *See* **930–999** **Form Divisions**

989   *See* **General Principles** xi **A** (2)

991–996   *See* **900's A**

Bibliography

The classifier will find in the following titles useful suggestions for manipulating the DC and illumination of the concepts on which it is based:

Akers, Susan Grey. *Simple library cataloging.* 4th ed. Chicago, American Library Association, 1954. p. 5–23: "Classification"

Bliss, Henry Evelyn. *The organization of knowledge in libraries and the subject-approach to books.* New York, H. W. Wilson, 1934. p. 193–229: "The Decimal classification"

Dewey, Harry. *An introduction to library cataloging and classification.* 4th ed. rev. & enl. Madison, Wis., Capital Press, 1957. Sections on the Decimal classification are scattered thruout

Dewey, Melvil. *Dewey decimal classification and relative index.* 16th ed. Lake Placid Club, N.Y., Forest Press, 1958. 2 v. (2439 p.)

———— *Dewey decimal classification and relative index.* 8th abr. ed. Lake Placid Club, N.Y., Forest Press, 1959. 495 p.

Eaton, F. Thelma. *Cataloging and classification; an introductory manual.* 2d ed. Champaign, Ill., Illini Union Bookstore, 1957. p. 64–75: "Dewey's Decimal classification scheme"

Herdman, Margaret May. *Classification; an introductory manual.* 2d ed. Chicago, American Library Association, 1947. p. 19–24: "Dewey decimal classification"

Illinois. University. Graduate School of Library Science. *The role of classification in the modern American library.* Champaign, Ill., Illini Union Bookstore, 1959. p. 62–75: "The enduring qualities of Dewey"

Mann, Margaret. *Introduction to cataloging and the classification of books.* 2d ed. Chicago, American Library Association, 1943. p. 44–67: "A classification schedule and the Decimal classification"

———— ———— 1st ed. Chicago, American Library Association, 1930. p. 383–393: "Cataloging and classifying history books"

Merrill, William Stetson. *Code for classifiers.* 3d ed. Chicago, American Library Association, 1954. 177 p.

Metcalfe, John Wallace. *Subject classifying and indexing of libraries and literature.* New York, Scarecrow Press, 1959. p. 15–17: "The Decimal classifications and the Dewey system." p. 132–140: "Number building in DC"

Mills, Jack. *A modern outline of library classification.* London, Chapman & Hall, 1960. p. 57–73: "The Decimal classification of Melvil Dewey"

Phillips, W. Howard. *A primer of book classification.* London, Association of Assistant Librarians, 1955. p. 64–93: "The Decimal classification." p. 180–203: "Practical application of book classification"

Savage, Ernest Albert. *Manual of book classification and display for public libraries.* London, Allen & Unwin, 1946. References to the Decimal classification are scattered thruout

Sayers, William Charles Berwick. *An introduction to library classification, theoretical, historical and practical with readings, exercises and examination papers.* 9th ed. London, Grafton, 1958. p. 114–135: "Decimal classification." p. 217–287: "A short course in practical classification with special reference to the Decimal classification"

———— *A manual of classification for librarians and bibliographers.* 3d ed. rev. London, Grafton, 1959. p. 111–126: "Decimal classification: The Dewey classification"

Tauber, Maurice Falcolm. *Classification systems.* New Brunswick, N.J., Graduate School of Library Service, Rutgers, the State University, 1961. p. 4–62: "Melvil Dewey and the Decimal classification"

————, ed. *Technical services in libraries: acquisitions, cataloging, classification, binding, photographic reproduction, and circulation opera-*

tions. New York, Columbia University Press, 1954. p. 190–199: "Dewey decimal classification"

U.S. Library of Congress. Decimal Classification Office. *Decimal classification additions, notes, and decisions.* Washington, Library of Congress, 1959–   . Volume 1, Number 1, January 1959–